LondonbyLondon

The
insiders'
guide

LondonbyLondon

Edited by Graham Pond

The
insiders'
guide

First published in Great Britain in 2005 by Friday Books
An imprint of The Friday Project Limited
83 Victoria Street, London SW1H 0HW

www.thefridayproject.co.uk
www.fridaybooks.co.uk

© 2005 The Friday Project Limited

British Library Cataloguing in Publication Data

A catalogue record for this book is available
from the British Library

ISBN 0 95483181 0

Design by Staziker Jones
www.stazikerjones.co.uk

Printed and bound by MWL Print Group
www.mwl.co.uk

The Publisher's policy is to use paper manufactured
from sustainable forests.

Illustrations by Greg Stekelman
www.themanwhofellasleep.com

Contents

Welcome to LondonbyLondon

Ah, London. So good they named it once, knowing that naming it twice would have been, frankly, a bit naff. What a city. What London doesn't have is most probably not worth having. Not counting a nice beach of course. A beach would be great. And maybe a couple of mountains. But apart from that, London has it all. It reminds us of that old joke by the American comedian, Steven Wright: 'You can't have everything. Where would you put it?' The answer of course – excepting seaside and mountainscapes – is London.

Another perhaps more practical question Steven might have posed is: 'You can't have everything. How on earth would you find something when you needed it?' This is a little trickier. Thankfully, *London by London: the insiders' guide* is here to help.

London by London began life in 2002, when a small group of Londoners – ten in fact – began sharing their special London secrets and asking for tips about the stuff they didn't know in a weekly email newsletter. LBL quickly proved an ideal way for Londoners to help each other to get the best out of the city.

The best thing about *London by London* is that it's written by real Londoners – and we're not talking Bow Bells or jellied eels here. We're talking about the people who live, work and play in London; from the people who ride the tubes to the people who drive the tubes, to the people who simply can't afford the tubes, but thankfully have still got access to a computer.

And there is no end to the stuff that these people know – whether it's where to get a decent cobra dumpling when you need one or basic tidal theory and its effect on the direction of the Thames; whether it's where to get a game of beach volleyball (even factoring in the absence of a beach) to the best places to make filthy whoopee in public, the collective knowledge of LBLers seems infinite.

Within the pages of this book you'll find the very best the London by London community has to offer – everything you need to make the most out of living in this city that never ever fails to surprise. Things you shouldn't miss; things you must avoid at all costs.

So whether you're new to London or you're covered head to toe in shiny buttons, boiled beef and carrots, come on in, pull up a pew and join the community. You know it makes sense.

London by London

And if you know something we don't, don't keep it to yourself. Share the knowledge. Join the LbL community and sign up for the weekly email at
www.londonbylondon.co.uk

Observations

Sometimes, with the weariness of the workaday world weighing heavy on your shoulders, it's easy to walk the streets of London with your eyes closed and your head up your arse. No one's blaming you. You're only human. Thankfully other Londoners are not quite so self-obsessed as you. They walk around with their eyes and many other orifices open wide, alive to the city and all its

bewildering captivating beauty and foulness. In this section they share the wealth of their knowledge, and often their ignorance, with you, the fortunate reader. The colourful characters, the guerrilla art, the squawking birds, the squeaking mice, the inspiring views and the inexplicable sounds. All human life is here, and more besides.

Londoners by Londoners

Identity

What makes a person a Londoner? Is it just that they live and work here? Or is it something more than just that? Can I kick things off by saying I live and work here as a British resident (the stamp in my passport says so), I have an Oyster card, I help little old drunk Irish ladies find their way home, I have a favourite local curry house, the staff at my local *Oddbins* now recognise me, I don't take the tube between Charing Cross and Embankment, I have a Nectar card, I'm a member of my local cinema and theatre, I can find my way from Regent's Park to Bankside without a map, and I get really cranky with people who don't let me off the train before trying to barge their way on. Does any of this count?

💬 JB

I think once you feel like a Londoner, you probably are one. It has nothing to do with where you come from so few of us actually are from London. Some people manage to get there, others don't: I know people from a number of countries who clearly act and feel like Londoners, but also know English people from outside the city who've been here for a while but never seem to act like they're really at home. Being a Londoner is a state of mind, and from your description I think you're already there.

💬 Jif

Well, seeing as you're not from London yet no doubt think that London is centre of the universe; have no wish to assimilate into other more interesting and potentially challenging English cities/towns, believe all the rubbish the transient media (mostly resident in London) feeds you, and use the grating term 'Londoner' unlike someone who grew up in Brixton or Hackney or whatever, then you DEFINITELY sound like a typical 'Londoner'. So what was the question again?

⌐ DB

Off

Riding up on the Wimbledon branch of the District line every morning is essentially a tedious experience, as is trying to get off the train at Earl's Court when it's typically rammed. But, occasionally at least, the journey is made more enjoyable by a middle-aged man who, when wanting to leave the train, adopts the odd tactic off saying 'Off, off, off, off, off, off, off, off, off, off, off' over and over again to his fellow passengers until he finally manages to step from the train.

I like him.

⌐ Spyrone

Character

A few years ago I worked in High Holborn, a place I found to be grey, overcrowded and depressing. My time there was made more entertaining by daily sightings of a colourful character I'd see walking around the area. It was this wee guy's clothes that made an instant impression; he'd always wear a grey wedding groom's-style top hat and pair of child's football shorts, regardless of the climate. He was only about 5ft high, and with his long curly hair and sharp features, he looked like a Mini-Me version of the magician/comedian Jerry Sadowitz. He was constantly muttering to himself and always seemed to be in a hurry somewhere. I assume he was a tramp, but for all I know he could've been an eccentric millionaire. Has anyone else seen the chap I'm describing? And most importantly, does anyone know what the guy really does?

💬 **Bunky**

I saw the little man you speak of getting off a Piccadilly line tube at Piccadilly Circus a few weeks ago. He had on short trousers (schoolboy style) and a jacket in a shiny grey material. Plus knee-high socks, pink shirt and hat. Thought I had spied a tube elf!

💬 **Beaver**

Further to Bunky's sighting of the colourful character in Holborn, has anyone espied the rather elderly, immaculately turned out chap who strides purposefully around the Rosebery Avenue area... rain or shine, winter or summer, always dressed in a dark pencil skirt and knee high red socks with matching red hat! He also has this faraway look on his face, as if yearning for his lost trousers...

🗨 Teefer

Sorry

Did anyone else see the young guy standing in a T-shirt (in the freezing cold) on Regent Street/Langham Place near the BBC at 8.30ish on Monday morning? He was holding a hitchhiker's card that had the single word 'SORRY' written on it.

First of all I thought this was for some Trigger Happy-style stunt, until I saw a car pull up next to him and a tearful young woman get out and hug him. They got back in the car and drove off happily, never to be seen again... The mind boggles as to what it was all about, but it was quite a sight all the same. I must admit to being a little moved myself. Anyone see this or know the full story?

🗨 Pete

London by looking

Shivers

When I first moved to London I had a load of mates who lived over in Mile End; my journey home to Clapham would involve making my way to Waterloo via Embankment. One night the tubes were messed up so I legged it across the river between the two stations what a buzz! That view sent shivers down my spine and really made me feel part of the city. Six years later I still always make a point of walking between those two stations. What places or situations have other LbLers found themselves in that have had the same effect?

🗨 Witness #01

The view that comes to mind through my mental cobwebs this morning is the view of the City of London as you enter Liverpool Street, just after Bethnal Green rail station. As you descend, the City springs up from the rest of the horizon like some 21st-century St Michael's Mount. Especially good early morning when the sun reflects off the glass façades... Don't get me wrong, this isn't a paean to a shrine of international capitalism, I just like the view.

🗨 SFULG

I used to have to go into work at 6am for several weeks every summer. I will never forget one bright morning coming over Westminster Bridge. There was not a cloud in the sky and the early morning sun was glinting off all the gilt on the Houses of Parliament. It was one of the most beautiful things I've seen and made me glad to live here.

🗨 MadKingSoup

Mine is the stretch of canal between London Fields and Primrose Hill. That stretch takes in London Fields, Shoreditch, Islington, Camden, Regents Park Zoo and Primrose Hill. Absolutely stunning, I cycled it last weekend and fell in love with London all over again.

🗨 Griff

I wholeheartedly agree with you, the view between Waterloo and Embankment is one of my favourites too and I have snapped it many times. Another view that I never get tired of is the view at Parliament Hill on Hampstead Heath and the view at Primrose Hill where you can sit back in the sunshine and admire the beautiful city we live in. Hoorah!

💬 **davina**

The one view of London that has stuck in my mind the most is one of a rainbow a few years ago. I saw it from the top deck of a 133 bus going over London Bridge after work. There's always brilliant skies in London, what with all the pollution (big 'god-rays' and extra pink sunsets) but this one took the biscuit. The sun was setting over Westminster, while it was raining over Docklands. The geometry of sun, rain and bus was such that the rainbow appeared to shine straight out of the peak of the Canary Wharf tower and curve symmetrically right over Tower Bridge before getting lost behind the GLA. I just dropped my jaw and stared. You'd have thought it was set up, the alignment was so perfect. I don't think I've seen a more beautiful combination of the city and nature.

When I turned back, I noticed that nobody else on the bus was looking up; all were buried in their *Evening Standard*s or yapping into a phone.

💬 **Crispy**

I still get a major thrill at the view of London all around me when I drive on the elevated section of the Westway coming in to central London.

💬 **RiverMan**

Grab a coffee by the Tower of London and jump on a boat to Greenwich. The views of ancient pubs (i.e. the leaning Captain Cook), strange dockland creations and beautiful churches (Shadwell in particular) at most times of the day are very cool and relaxing... and they move.

💬 **BillyGoat**

Wednesday morning, walking from London Bridge to St Paul's in the rain, the *Globe*, *Tate Modern*, *Vinopolis*, the Millennium Bridge and a smile from a pretty girl. I LOVE London.

💬 **Wonderferret**

Lights

I live at Canary Wharf, and looking out towards the city/Soho at night recently I've spotted spotlights 'dancing' on the clouds. I can see them at the time of writing, and also saw them in the early hours of last night. Anyone know who/why/what they're for? Google didn't come up with anything, mainly 'cos I wasn't able to tell it whereabouts they're based.

💬 **Natts**

I thought it was some dodgy nightclub really really going for it, but then reasoned that not even the most hardcore of establishments could still be going a week later. After lighting a special candle, changing into a midnight blue velvet cloak and ingesting some mystical substances, I consulted my Tarot cards, a couple of unlucky chickens and some pieces of thrice-blessed willow, and they gave me the following answer, which remarkably was the same as the one that Google came up with just now. The lights come from the lasers at each end of Oxford Street that are part of the Christmas lights and also London's Olympic bid.

🗨 ChildoftheJago

Balls

On a 168 bus the other day I noticed small black 7" balls with spikes coming out at all angles, fixed on the lampposts around Holborn. I have since noticed the same thing in silver along around Camden Market. They have their own power supply and they look like fibre optic lights but they're already on streetlights... it is driving me insane not knowing why.

🗨 Ali

I have worked around Holborn for a couple of years. Around Christmas time my colleagues and I noticed the fibre optic ball thingies being installed and thought, ho hum, politically correct Christmas decorations, completely lacking any meaning.

However, they have stayed, and we have no idea why. Not really the answer to the question, I know, but it's nice to know other people are mulling over the same London things.

🗨 anon

I saw white ones the other day I think in Holborn, I thought how pretty they looked, but also thought they might just be left over from Christmas.

🗨 Spandangle

I can't for the life of me remember where I read this, but apparently these Christmas-like decorations are put up in high crime areas because they reduce people's inclination to commit felonies! Similarly, studies have shown reductions in crime when classical music is played over loudspeakers at train stations, and that practice can now been seen throughout the world.

💬 pdr

Art

Whilst travelling into town on 8th December on the top deck of the 243, I was very amused to see that some guerrilla art has been installed on top of various bus shelters along Old Street. I spotted filled cereal bowls with open pints of milk, turf complete with dog poo, a sign saying 'are you sure?'. Anyone else spot them? Anyone know what they're all about?

💬 Dolly

There is also guerrilla art along the 55 and the number 8 route, along Hackney Road and Bethnal Green Road respectively. These ones are simply pieces of chipboard with 'Eine' on them. Eine appears to be a collective along the same lines as Basta and others that are prolific in the East End.

💬 Griff

Eine: This is a graf/urban artist who was featured at the Santa's Ghetto exhibition along with artists like Banksy, Jamie Hewlett (drew Gorillaz), Chris Cunningham (directed Aphex Twin, Leftfield, Portishead vids). Eine typically favours smiley faces in his printed work.

💬 Jayc

Wheels

Is it just me, or is there an increasing number of unicyclists on London's streets these days?

🗨 **magpie**

I haven't noticed the increasing numbers of unicyclists but there do seem to be more and more of those curious reclining bicycles. Are they called recumbents? Or have I just invented that? Is there any point to these things beyond being an expression of their riders', um, quirky personalities? (And being supremely unmanoeuvrable in even slightly heavy car or pedestrian traffic.)

🗨 **PhilG**

Yes, they are called recumbents. My aunt is partially disabled and uses a recumbent tricycle. Apparently they are easier to pedal and stuff. So all those people are probably disabled or lazy.

🗨 **Recumbent Guy**

Sign

Does anyone out there know the meaning of the small cardboard signs lashed to streetlights, signposts and other upright objects in the city centre? They're often arrow-shaped and appear to have codes on like 'BII LOC' or 'BABY COW', which I've heard is Steve Coogan's TV production company. Are they directions for film crews or something? They tend to be near busy roads, but the odd one crops up down quiet side streets...

🗨 **JJ**

The little cardboard signs that you see on London lampposts are known as Unit Signs and are most often there to indicate to film crews, cameramen, caterers etc. the way to their filming location. They can apply to movies or TV programmes that are being filmed. It used to be that location managers just put the word UNIT on the signs so the general public didn't know what was being filmed but that got a bit silly with all the stuff going on in London at one time so now they give it away by putting the names of the show.

💬 reetyre

Crane

 Does anyone know what the *massive* floating crane is doing moored up near Tower Bridge? It is an object of fascination for me on my walk to work. It looks like a floating Battersea Power Station or some sort of mobile oil rig.

💬 Clefty

The crane is actually a floating wind farm installation factory for making off shore wind farms. I think it is doing some installation up North somewhere, but they have brought it to London as a marketing exercise basically, to show it off to potential clients that can't be bothered to travel to look at it. The sticking up bits actually slide downwards to make legs that sit on the ocean floor. It can withstand waves of up to 45 feet or something. I read about it in the *Metro*.

💬 Metro Geek

Reading by London

Metro

Have any real people actually written to *Metro*
our esteemed freebie lately? Its letters page
seems to have turned into the *Daily Mail*; recently
homeless (they earn more than we do you know),
immigrants (see previous), the disabled (aren't they brave),
gay and Asian policemen (aren't they disgusting) all get a
mention. I need to know if this is somehow representative
of New London. If so should I be planning to move?
If not can we start a campaign to get normal lefty
liberalism restored?

Mike (Mrs)

I've written in to *Metro* before, saying things I didn't
believe using the names of people I don't like. Maybe there's
a lot of that goes on? I'm sure in most magazines friends
of the letters editor provide content. I had two letters in
the same issue of one music mag. Can anyone else provide
a backup to the theory it's all stinking and corrupt?

Pauly

Anyone in PR knows how easy it is to get letters
published in newspapers and the unscrupulous in the trade
send in fake letters from imaginary members of the public
to back up their campaign/company. But this bizarre feature
of the *Metro* probably just reflects that people with a
beef (V. Meldrew) are more likely to promote their opinion
than people who are generally OK with things. Be interesting

for LbLers to test the theory and report results here.
More likely to get printed too if they are short and direct.

              💬 **Dave**

Originally when the *Metro* started up it was an independent
paper then the *Daily Mail* paid LU to run it for them. Since
then it's gone more like the *Daily 'Hate'*. I don't even know
why I pick it up in the morning these days as I generally can't
be arsed to read more than the headlines of the paper. I
think London Underground should put a stop to it.

              💬 **Not a NIMBY**

Thought

**For some months now, Oval station has had a
'Thought For The Day' displayed on the board
that usually says things like 'Northern line
suspended between etc. etc.' This started out as
usually trite, irritating platitudinous bollocks like
'A smile costs nothing' blah de blah, but recently,
it's becoming increasingly morbid and depressive.
This is what the merry commuters of
Oval/Kennington were treated to this morning:**

Colours blind the eye
Sounds deafen the ear
Flavours numb the taste
Thoughts weaken the mind
Desires wither the heart

Er, okay. Thanks!

              💬 **bad girl bubby**

London by London by London

Just reading the London by London book and chuckling on a packed Piccadilly when a lady next to me actually asked me what I was reading! I do believe the first non-beggar to actually speak to me in nearly three years in London on the tube! So I just passed the book, and told her to get online! No badge required!

⌐ **Tonytone**

Bugger me! I just saw someone wearing an LbL badge! A tiny little blonde girl (really a blonde lady not a child although she was very small), wearing a brown leather coat, going down the escalator at Holborn tube. I was going up the other escalator at the time so couldn't stop to say hello which is a shame because she seemed like a very nice, happy person and an LbLer. How cool is that!? And annoyingly I wasn't wearing my badge. I won't leave home without it again!

⌐ **Matt A**

I was very excited to receive my copy of the LbL book the other day but slightly concerned with the free pin badge. Did anyone else receive a perfect imitation of a 45 Colt Magnum? It wasn't until I rotated it 45 degrees to the left that all was revealed!

⌐ **scally**

Yesterday I went to Borders and bought two copies of the LbL book. One for my boyfriend's brother and one for my best friend. Anyway, I was walking from Oxford Street to Bond Street tube, when I saw the Sinners and Winners Man. How cool would it be if I got him to sign my newly purchased LbL books?? Very cool but I chickened out.

⌐ **Beryl Bouffe Schwede**

Bang

Just after Christmas I received the LbL badge
and have been wearing the pin with pride on my
jacket. A few people have asked what it's about,
and I quite like telling them, directing them to the
website, and sounding quite knowledgeable about
London. Well, I went to the US on business recently,
without thinking to remove the badge; hey,
there might even be someone who'd heard of LbL
and we could exchange banter about the Sinners
and Winners Man...

When killing time, browsing in a book shop in
Washington airport, the lady from the shop called
over. Horrified at the fact that people speak to
strangers over there with more than a grunt (too
much time on the tube) I looked slightly aghast.
Then she said 'hey man, I see you like your 45
nice work!' No idea what she was talking about.
She pointed at my LbL badge. It had inadvertently
slipped round about 90 degrees clockwise, and the
shouting tube thing had unwittingly become the
butt of a serious pistol, in her mind's eye at least
you see what you're looking for.

She then pointed two fingers at me, looking
down the barrel of her arm, and did that awful
thumb-click-pull-the-trigger thing, with the
appropriate noise, of course. I was slightly
embarrassed that I'd been isolated by the shop
assistant, even before she'd heard my 'quaint'
accent. I then had to explain to the (clearly

Republican) gun-toting yokel that, actually it was a pin badge for an internet club in London, without sounding like I was part of some underground hacker network. A tricky position indeed. I got away with a couple of non-committal responses to questions of how neat London was, but I had to get out of there. Next, she'd be offering me membership of her clan or something. Somehow I managed to extricate myself from the situation, by grabbing the nearest magazine, thrusting some money in her direction, and backing out of the shop. What we LbLers go through, just for the badge...

☐ Lifelonglondoner

Eenistennit

Has anyone noticed how old many of the *Evening Standard* sellers are? There's an old woman by St Paul's station who is all hunched over and looks about 70, and I've seen lots of others. My favourite is the guy that is (used to be?) by Camden station. He had been shouting 'Standard' for so many years that it just came out as an incomprehensible noise. What will happen when these old people die off? Is there a new generation of sellers ready to take their place, or is standing outside in all weathers for a pittance not really that appealing to anyone now?

☐ Crouch Ender

Surely the *Standard* sellers fulfil a role much like those who sell ice cream in the south of Spain. It would appear that you have to be a nonagenarian if you wish to receive a licence to sell

frozen dairy products, particularly in Andalusia and Almeria.
Or perhaps that says more about Spanish bureaucracy and how
long people wait for the wheels of government to move. Having
said that, there are also many very young *Standard* sellers
around the Moorgate and Liverpool Street areas. Some so
young as to warrant the old question of interfering middle-age:
'Why aren't you at school, sonny Jim?'

💬 psaf

Grammar

 **Anyone know why Barons Court has no
apostrophe (unlike the next station on the line,
Earl's Court)?**

💬 jif

Ooh, I know this one. Finally, carrying around that collection
of useless facts about the Underground pays off.

If we're going to be all grammatical about things, Earl's Court
should actually be Earls' Court, named as it was for the joint
manorial court of the Earls of Warwick and Holland. You can see
their influence in plenty of local street names, and I'm sure one
of the lords of the manor would be chuffed to bits that his
legacy is now the location of the 24-hour Tesco. Barons Court,
on the other hand, is home to some very horrible pubs, a lot
of PR girl flatshares, and absolutely no Barons whatsoever,
then or now. It is an entirely made-up name, the equivalent
of 'Sunny Meadows Estate' (What meadow? Where? Under all
these houses?) and 'Sea View Cottage' (in Derbyshire). I'm sure
I remember reading somewhere that the developer who bought
the land adjacent to the Earl's Court area fancied giving his

new housing development a posh-sounding name like its
neighbour, something that called to mind stately living hence,
Barons Court, and apostrophes be damned.

For a change, it's not LU's fault that one has an
apostrophe and the other doesn't. Now, St. James's Park
is another matter entirely...

💬 **Mrs Beck**

Regarding the apostrophe debate of Earl's Court etc., TFL
can't make their mind up (well, there's a surprise). At different
points of the station, Earl's Court is spelt with and without
an apostrophe! Proof was shown on the wonderful ITV1
programme *The Great British Spelling Test* recently. (I say
wonderful, only because I was the annoying git who walked
away with the £10,000 first prize!)

💬 **robram**

Nature by London

Tube Mice

**Tube mice! Where are they? Just two years ago I
remember getting all gooey-eyed over two sweet little
balls of fur squabbling over a gnawed KFC scrap on the
Bakerloo line platform at Piccadilly Circus. You could tell
who the young ones were, because they actually had a tail.
And you could always guarantee seeing a gang of them in a
West End tube station. Now, nothing. Not a squeak. Have they
exterminated the little rascals?**

💬 **Fleance**

It's funny you were wondering where all the tube mice have gone, because only yesterday I was waiting for my train at Piccadilly Circus station when, to my delight, I spotted one near the tunnel. It warmed my heart to see that it was as it should be: tail-less.

💬 **Cornholio**

I love the little scrappers! I'm intrigued by their dirty, scary life and that the fact of it doesn't diminish their enthusiasm for really lame scraps. Always raises a smile on my weary commute.

💬 **magpie**

On the subject of tube mice, I see them around all the time but I often wonder whether they are the colour they are because they have evolved to blend in with the rails, or whether they 're just really dirty. In short: what colour would a tube mouse be if you gave him a wash?

💬 **Audrey**

I don't know where the mice have moused off too, but I do remember having a (rare!) stupid moment:

M: 'Why do you think they're black?'

X: 'Huh?'

M: 'Well, from a Darwinian point of view, what benefit do they have in being black...?'

X: 'Mate...'

M: 'I mean, there is nothing apparently hunting them, so even if they were bright pink, it wouldn't make the slightest bit of difference!'

X: 'Mate...'

M: 'Seriously, think about it...'

X: 'Mate?'
M: 'Yeah?'
X: 'They're just dirty.'
M: 'Oh. Oh, yeah.'
D'oh.

💬 **mudge**

What's really interesting about the mice is it seems that they *have* evolved into special tube mice. I used to work for the Northern line many years ago and the wife of the manager of the line had done some research and discovered that mice on different lines had evolved/mutated as suitable for their lines, e.g. they are born deaf on the very old, loud, lines this would make sense as the life cycle of the mouse is not very long and a deaf mouse would have an easier time of it than a hearing one.

In case you're getting smart alecky, vibration would let them know when a train was coming. They eat leftover food etc, but there's probably also a lot of nutrition for a mouse in the discarded hair and skin that has to be cleared off the lines she also wrote (and possibly illustrated) a children's book about mice on the line (this would be early '90s at a guess). More research is clearly needed.

💬 **Skidoo**

I can assure Fleance that our furry friends have not left the Underground. As a driver on the Piccadilly line, I laugh so much when I see people pointing at the mice running around as I arrive in a platform. Some seem very concerned that we might run the mice over but they are well gone by the time we get there. Also that the numbers that you see on the platform are only a small fraction of how many are in the tunnels. You are never alone!

PS. Can I ask people not to try and 'thumb' a lift as I
enter a platform. You may think it's the first time I've seen
it but it certainly isn't. Thank you.

⌨ **Dream Monkey**

Rat

**Just come back from first trip to New York and while
I'm now sort of guiltily in love with that city (like
having an affair behind my beloved London's back)
I have to say I thought the subway was shocking.
OK, so it's pretty efficient and runs all night but my
God, the smell, the dripping ceilings, the corroding
metal and ew! The rats! Big effing rats! One ran right
in front of me in broad daylight, which apparently
happens all the time. Will make me think twice
about moaning about the tube. It may not be perfect,
but at least it's dry and the rodents are small.**

⌨ **mindtherat**

Nightbirds

**Was kept awake in N7 last night (6/12) by evil birds
singing through the early hours (definitely at 1am
and 3am) does anyone know why? Surely this is
against nature I thought they were supposed to**
sleep when it is dark. Was not a wine-induced dream as
my boyfriend also heard them.

⌨ **tk**

I too live in N7, tk, and the bloody birds keep going off at
3am. My local councillor, clearly after votes, as keeps visiting,

tells me it's because the trains have stopped running that we can hear them. I'd love to have trains running out of Finsbury Park at 3am, but never happened since I've been there.
The next reason that he gave was that it was 'young hooligans' on their way home from the pub. When I asked where that late licence pub was, so I could have a great night out, he couldn't tell me. Anyone out there know the real reason the birds keep singing at 3am in N7?

💬 **Claire**

I live in Holloway N19 and have also noticed birdsong in the early hours of the morning, 1am etc. Way too early for dawn. I've never noticed it before but now they've been singing their hearts out every night and it's unsettling. It makes you think it's time to wake up not go to sleep. Anyone got any ideas why birds suddenly start to sing at night?!

💬 **Red**

If the nocturnal bird song was loud, persistent, with regularly changing, quite complex passages, with a hint of humour, chances are it's a song thrush. And that it'll keep going for several weeks. They start claiming territory quite early in the cycle. The good news? It's a harbinger of longer daylight hours. Only way to stop it singing is to shoot it.

💬 **Jezza, Highbury**

The reason birds can be heard trilling at ungodly hours in N17 (and I can also vouch for N4) is that particularly bright night time street lighting fools them into thinking it's daylight, ergo confused 3am bursts of song... my mate has christened them 'Tweetie-bastards'.

💬 **Hettie**

Water

Every day on my trudge across London Bridge I look down at the murky water of the Thames below and frown because the damn thing's flowing in the wrong direction. Is this the first sign of a psychosis or has anyone else noticed how the Thames appears to flow upstream? Please come to my rescue with a plausible explanation before I jump in to test the currents.

🗨 fluffy mark

Quite basic tidal theory here... the gravitational pull of the moon combined with the daily rotation of the earth means there are (roughly) two tides a day, causing the water level to go both up and down twice. For the level to go up (a.k.a. the flood), water has to generally flow upstream (i.e. westerly inwards from the sea), and for the level to go down (a.k.a. the ebb), the water has to flow downstream (i.e. easterly out to the sea).

So, at the moment, your 'trudge' must be taking placing during the flood (i.e. the transition from low tide to high tide), though as the tides are determined by the moon (which orbits the earth every 28 days, independently of the earth rotating every 24 hours), you should soon find that the phasing of the tides will have advanced enough so that you will start to witness the ebb instead (high tide to low tide) at the same time of day.

🗨 Dave

Dave's on the money with what he says. Although what is less well known is that the Thames being tidal is a relatively new thing. These days the Thames from its estuary out east, through the Pool of London up to Twickenham lock is known as the 'Tideway' two tides a day (well, two high tides every 25 hours). The tidal lock at Twickenham (which you can see from the A316 as you head south-west out of town), is open two hours either side of high tide, which makes the stretch upriver of there, as far as Teddington Lock, semi-tidal.

The river has only been tidal in the last couple of hundred years, though, following the development of the flood plains, river banks and embankment areas in the last few centuries. Before then, when the sea's tide came in, the extra water in the estuary would flood the salty marshlands of Essex and Kent. Over the years, these were built on and the waters repelled, but the natural mass of water had to go somewhere and, instead, it was funnelled up the artificial river banks of the newly walled in and developed river.

The height difference between low and high tides can be quite marked as you head west. If you go to Putney, Hammersmith or Chiswick, for example, it can be as much as 10 metres of height or 4050 yards of foreshore. Which entertains the locals as those not in the know park their cars, only to return at high tide with, at best, a damp carpet, at worst, a flooded write-off.

💬 loaf

Maybe we could start an LbL prize for most condescending reply of the week? I nominate joyless fun-Nazi Dave... Speaking of tidal flows, did anyone read Blake Morrison's recent(ish) piece about his descent into London's sewer system? An interesting statement: 'Thames Water opens London's sewers for a week in May but prefers not to

advertise the fact too widely, for fear the demand would
be too great.'

Has anyone been? If so, what was it like? And, most
importantly, did they see any giant alligators?

🗩 **Tiddles**

I've not been down the London sewers, but a good friend
of mine is an environmental engineer and had the pleasure
last summer. The photos are amazing there are what can
only described as vaults as large as cathedrals down there
and the brickwork is phenomenal (God, I sound like such
an anorak). My mate walked practically from Angel to Bank
underground and raved about it for days. Perhaps worth
a trip, although the rumours of alligators and ninja turtles
do kind of put me off...

🗩 **WelshBird**

London by loondon

Rapunzel

I commute on the Bakerloo, changing at Oxford
circus on to the Central line. Not every day, but every
now and again, a smile comes across my face as
I trudge down the steps into the linking tunnel
between the two lines, as I hear the faint wailing of the
weird gypsy busker woman (I'm sure she has a proper
name like Leaf or Rapunzel).

Know who I mean? First, you hear a sort of yowling,
like a spurned lover pining for her ex, then the distant
strum of her guitar (with no apparent link with the timing

or sounds emanating from her mouth).Then, you see her
at the top of the slope at the junction of the tunnel to the
Victoria line. A tiny figure with a huge bow in her hair,
spindly stick legs (complete with thick white fishnets) and
a selection of costume jewellery. She has these doily-type
fingerless 'gloves' too, which are simply ridiculous.

An hilarious caricature of a woman, masquerading as
a busker. She would not look out of place on *Little Britain*.
A smattering of coppers on her guitar case is all the company
she keeps. Now this is all fine, but the most bizarre thing?
She has a CD on the floor for sale! Who let her record this?
Does she really think people might want to pay for this
noise? She must earn something there, or wouldn't carry
on doing it? Are you the one responsible for continuing this
morning mayhem? I heard that since the Carling Live thing
started on Underground stations, buskers had to audition?!
Either the people handing out licences are tone-deaf mutes,
or simply taking the proverbial Michael. If you can shed any
light on this lady, I'd love to know. Maybe you hired her for
some background musak at your wedding?!

💬 **Lifelonglondoner**

You've made me smile, Lifelonglondoner. I've been smirking
at that 'busker' for a good year or two now. I can't quite
understand why she persists in doing it; why anyone would
buy one of her CDs is beyond me. Mind you, thinking
about hippy woman has transformed my otherwise miserable
day. She sounds like an out-of-tune bastard offspring of
Joan Baez and Joni Mitchell but far worse than anyone could
ever imagine, if they had never heard her. Does she ever
sing on any other line? I thought the 'Carling' buskers were

meant to move stations, rather than always have the same
pitch? And was she one of the buskers featured on that
execrable CD *Sounds Of The Underground* that was released
about a month or so ago? Total rubbish!

robram

I've been asking around, and apparently she did time
(for that is what it must have felt like for the poor people
as they passed her) in the tunnel by South Ken. I can only
assume that the posh locals got her kicked out. Still tempted
to buy a CD from her just to see her reaction. I think she'd
probably faint. Maybe if five well-meaning LbLers bought
one, she'd go away?

Lifelonglondoner

Gross

**I normally get off at Holborn tube of a morning,
however, I fancied a change today and got off at
Covent Garden. Never again. The reason being Loyd
Grossman's nauseating voice talking to us all in the
lift telling us to visit the various attractions that CG
has to offer. This is not what I want to hear at any
time, let alone first thing in the morning. Why Loyd
Grossman? He's not even English, let alone a
Londoner! Who decides these things? I can only
think that he must have been cheap.**

Caroline

Grab

Yesterday I noticed that Lambeth Police had put up signs on Clapham Common Southside warning people not to use their phones on that stretch of road as nasty people on bikes were grabbing them out of people's hands as they went past. I made a mental note not to use my phone there anymore.

Bleary eyed this morning at 7.40am on my way to work I promptly forgot and rang my sister (strangeciara, look in your last *London by London* book under 'Water on the Underground'!). I looked up just at the right moment to see this bloke hurtling towards me at great speed on a bike. Alarm bells rang from the depths of my cobwebbed consciousness and I ducked out of the way. He took a swipe, thankfully missed my phone, but managed to whack me in the head in the process. I am still in shock, nothing a few drinks tonight won't sort out, but I thought I'd better warn all you lovely non-criminals to BEWARE! They missed my phone, but you might not be so lucky. I urge anyone who has had a similar brush with one of these bastards to let us all know and hammer it in to our brains that although most of us are nice people who help old ladies cross streets, there are others out there who are after your shiny new possessions and don't mind a bit of GBH in the process. Take care people!

🗨 Laferge

This has been happening for a long time near Clapham North station too. My cousin got grabbed, her phone and bag stolen and a nasty black eye in the process.

🗨 Emma

It's not just on your neck of the woods, it happened to
me on my street in W12 in the middle of the day. I got
off with a scratch and a knock on the head (they got the
phone) but the same happened to a friend of mine who
was beaten up when he wouldn't let go. Again, kids on bikes.
The cops said they get a £10 blim of hash for your phone;
somehow that doesn't make me feel better. I know people
say it all the time but DON'T USE YOUR PHONE ON THE
STREET, it's really upsetting when you get mugged.
It's put me right off my own street but that's not hard,
I do live in Shepherd's Bush...

💬 **handsfree**

The same happened to me a couple of years ago outside
the *Museum of Childhood* in Bethnal Green. Furious at
having my head walloped and my phone nicked, I took chase
up the road in rush hour and thought I'd spotted my man.
I immediately launched into a torrent of verbal abuse and
demanded my phone back. The young man waiting on his
bike stared at me and asked if I was serious. I promptly
burst into tears and walked away. Very cool (by the way
if it was you, dear reader, sorry about that I didn't even
have the presence of mind to apologise). To top it off this
was the second time my phone had gone awol in two weeks
and CarphoneShitHouse decided not to insure me anymore.
Be careful of the little sods.

💬 **Miss Lake**

Recorder

 I was just wondering if anyone has seen the man in the wheelchair on Oxford Street who plays the recorder and only knows one note? Do people really give him money?

💬 **crackers**

Sadly he is there regularly, getting in the ear of people popping into *Debenhams* over the lunch period. I think it's a whistle and rather alarmingly I actually saw someone throw money in his pot last week (no doubt in the hope he'll shut up).

💬 **Pussycat**

I would not be so quick to judge that the guy only knows one note. During numerous enforced shopping trips to Oxford Street spent waiting/sulking/smoking by my boyfriend outside shops, he has become convinced that the guy is actually creating a masterpiece. It's just in a different time frame to the one you or I think in. Apparently the guy plays a different note each week (I mean who would notice?)... so if you recorded him over, say, five years, you'd have the first movement of his symphony...

💬 **Juicy**

I did actually think of LbL the other day when I saw a guy either at Tottenham Court Road or Oxford Street. He wasn't in a wheelchair but I remember thinking of how crap he sounded. Don't mean to offend the poor guy because I certainly couldn't have done better well at least on the recorder. I'm sure I could've burped a better tune though.

💬 **MrMINI**

Radio

Who is the strange-looking hairy man who always stands around Manor House with a small radio, shouting about Arsenal and worryingly sometimes brandishing a baby's bottle? Everyone who has ever passed through Manor House must have seen him!

💬 talkative

I know exactly who you mean, although I don't know much about the strange hairy man. He has been loitering around Manor House for years, dressed from head to toe in Arsenal merchandise. I remember him from my school days, We used to call him 'Babies Bottle' due to him offering it to us as we walked past him! Freaky!

💬 sweetcheeks

Surprise surprise, he's probably just another homeless man with mental health problems. Why don't you talk to him, find out his name, and then contact social services to see if he's gone missing from a Care in the Community program? Alternatively you could carry on smirking into your copy of the *Life of Pi* and wait for the police to move him on next time he shits himself.

💬 Baastaard

LBL greatest hits: the sinners and winners man

The admirably dedicated Scouse evangelist on Oxford Street can also be heard at various London music events, seemingly harbouring a particular prejudice against festival-goers. At the last Essential festival he took to haranguing the circular queue for the free buses when a couple of wags decided simply to follow him all the around the circle, pulling faces and giggling. Some distinctly un-Christian kicking ensued. Also, a mate of mine, slightly the worse for wear one morning, told him to fuck off, at which point he explained that whilst a servant of God, he wasn't averse to giving profane unbelievers a good kicking. I'm presuming this irritating individual is a freelancer; anyone know if any particular group is unlucky enough to have him as a member?

🗨 Tim

What most people don't know is that the religious nut used to think he was a werewolf and would occasionally get on London news reports because he would beg the police to lock him up come every full moon. Then he found God, or more specifically a cassette tape of some preacher that he constantly listens to and repeats out loud (you'd think he'd remember the words by now).

🗨 Giz

The evangelist fundamentalist Scouser once let rip into a megaphone about four inches from my ear, just by Selfridges. As I'm an opera singer my aural health is crucial to my living, so I lifted my music folder between my head and his instrument of torture. This earned me roaring chastisement as 'spawn of Satan', no less, which as a gay, liberal, Anglo-Catholic I consider a compliment from his ilk. But if anyone has a water pistol...

💬 **Maxbiker**

I first encountered the Sinners and Winners scouse preacher man on the Northern line about a year ago. He was walking along asking people if they 'were believers' and when they said 'No' or ignored him he told them they were going to hell. I am a Christian, so when he asked me if I was a believer I said, 'Yes', and told him that I didn't think he had the right to tell people they were going to hell. He proceeded to tell me that I was evil and that the devil was in me etc. I asked him how he knew that seeing as he didn't know me at all and we had only exchanged a few brief words. 'God's told me,' he answered. (Great answer.) He went on to tell me how the Pope, the Queen and the Archbishop of Canterbury are all going to hell. I asked him who was going to heaven then... just him? God's chosen messenger? I never found out his answer, because as the doors opened at the next tube stop, he ran down the carriage and away. I confess to having shouted 'wanker' at him as he jumped off the train. Slapped wrists there. And that's his problem; he knows nothing about Christianity, or at least if he does, he preaches and practises little of it. It's people like him who give the majority of perfectly normal Christians a bad name.

What we need is a 6'5" body-building priest with a megaphone. That way, they can actually have a serious debate with no chance of him being able to kick back. I'd watch it.

💬 **Dr Bone**

The religious zealot that has been mentioned a fair bit recently used to stand in the tunnels of South Kensington tube station complete with megaphone and annoying attitude. Eventually he would leave, but it usually took the intervention of the British Transport Police. He can become quite violent when challenged.

One amusing incident stands out in my mind from last summer. One of the Revenue protection staff went over to him and asked him to leave. He refused and stood his ground. The RPI again asked him to leave and the conversation became quite loud and heated. The nut then starts throwing his arms around wildly announcing that he preaches for God. The RPI replied 'I'm sure you do sir, but I box four times a week, now fuck off.' He did.

💬 Jon

Update

So I was passing time on Saturday afternoon at Oxford Circus where I couldn't help but overhear the Sinners and Winners man as he berated the passing public for spending money on frivolities and not supporting starving children. Anyway, to my utter shock and horror, two policemen rocked up in a panda car, and moved in for the kill. He was eventually taken away by them, but that's not the reason for my writing. In the proceedings, I discovered his name. For years I've held true to the notion that it would be something strong and biblical Daniel, Jonah, Ezekiel, even Adam or Matthew. But no his name is Neil. Hey ho.

💬 WelshBird

WelshBird is wrong in the b3ta interview, Sinners and
Winners man clearly says his name is Phil. If anyone didn't
go to read the interview, it's very good; it's easy to dismiss
him as a complete loony but the interview gives a lot of
background and he's obviously pretty intelligent and has
a very interesting story.

 Crouch Ender

Did anyone see the *Three Minute Wonder* slot after the
C4 news this week? Wednesday featured the Sinners and
Winners man. It made my week. I am a sinner with no
intention of becoming a winner, but I'm glad he cares enough
about all of us to stand at Oxford Circus day in day out.

 ruby ru

Sinners redux

**Sinners and Winners, Oxford Street's favourite
fundamentalist. We all now seem to know more
about him than his own mother does (thanks LbL).
For a short while though, there was a contender to
his crown; at least it seemed that way to me and
I'm looking for confirmation on this.**

**A tubby Greek (possibly Middle Eastern) looking guy,
in his mid thirties, immaculately, if tastelessly, dressed
in shiny slacks, shiny collarless shirt done up to top
button, strange gold decorative necklace thing, long
shiny jacket and a pair of the shiniest, slickest looking
loafers ever seen on a man. He seemed to work on
the principle that shininess was next to godliness.**

**He clutched what looked like a bible in his hand
and paced, head down, around Oxford Street, until**

some inner voice told him to latch onto someone. He would then scream religious-sounding gibberish at them, in a highly agitated state, for as long as they stayed within his range, before abruptly breaking off and recommencing his pacing, waiting for the next congregation to come his way.

I don't know how he chose his victims, seeing as he never seemed to look them in the face, maybe he judged them by the state of their footwear, the least shiny the closer to Satan. Can anyone back me up on this? This was a good year ago, for a period of a couple of months. Maybe there was a face off between him and Sinners and Winners, with Phil utilising his army training to dispatch him back to wherever he came from...

🖵 Dirtos

And finally

Name

Can someone please explain to me why more and more LbLers are leaving posts with ridiculous nicknames? It started off with the odd 'Kettle-Kisser' here, or '2kool4U Toff' there, but now it's got out of hand. I just simply do not understand why people choose these aliases, do you really think you're being cool or regaining your youth? Grow up.

🖵 Oliver Lester

Easy Tiger, I mean Oliver... what's in a name? We don't get to choose our real names; they're the virtual equivalent of bare skin. Our LbL suits allow us to cover our nakedness, so to speak. To frolic in virtual finery, of the binary nature. In fact, today I'm wearing my effyoo suit. What do you think, does my bum look big in this?

⌨ Zero Gravitas aka Vanessa

Someone has had a sense-of-humour bypass. I say the more ridiculous nicknames on LbL, the better it makes it all a bit like a CB radio community and I, for one, thought Smokey and the Bandit was brilliant. And, you never know, Oliver, perhaps some of the people posting here really are (a) 'cool' or (b) young. It is London, after all... 10–4, good buddy! (I'm posting under my real name.)

⌨ Cardinal Richelieu

Oh my God you're so right! How dare we choose these frivolous alter egos instead of a nice sensible name? I can only follow in your oh-so-grown-up footsteps. In future, I too will be known as Oliver Lester, and can only hope that all other LbLers can find the maturity to follow our lead and become Olivers too.

⌨ Oliver Lester

Food and Drink

What in God's name was going through Jacques Chirac's gnarled old head when he said that, after Finland, England was 'the country with the worst food'? One thing's for sure well, two, but the first is just rude. Jacques Chirac has obviously never sought the advice of London by Londoners before a culinary night on the town. If he had, he'd have known that the food in London is actually the finest in the world, even if only by dint of the fact that we steal the best that every other country has to offer. As a result, London has it all: Dutch, Polish, Mexican, Swiss, Vietnamese, Ethiopian; puddings, pastries, pasties and pies. Oh, and pubs. And pea fritters. And if you're really, really lucky, a nice bit of snake too. Mmmmmm. Tuck in.

London by carnivores

Snake

A few of us discussing snakes the other day, as you do, eventually came to the intersection of cobra and dinner. I had a hunch that there's some Chinese restaurant somewhere in this city where you can eat a snake, and I'd like to try it. Any ideas? Where can I dine on a boa?

💬 **Adderface**

I'm not sure you're going to find snake to eat in London. There used to be a restaurant called Edible which did all sorts of weird things, including ant mash and cobra sausages but it closed down a while back. Which suggests you may not really be missing out. Try Bangkok.

💬 **Little G**

I'm reliably informed that you'll have to go to Hong Kong or Vietnam to get some snake, mainly served shredded into glutinous soup. You won't find it in the UK.

💬 **Uptown Coil**

I've never been there so this info is second-hand, but I hear that *Archipelago* cooks all manner of weird and wonderful creatures for your culinary pleasure. This includes things like, erm, well, I don't really know: lion? hippo? duck-billed platypus? Anything really. Definitely zebra and alligator (or was it crocodile?) Anyway, I don't know for sure that they do snake, but it might be worth giving them a bell to ask.

They're somewhere in Fitzrovia I believe, quite possibly on Charlotte Street or thereabouts.

🗩 **WorldGirl**

Give *Champor Champor* (it's an, ahem, 'Malay Asian fusion restaurant') a call. It's near Guys Hospital at London Bridge and is excellent. In the past they've served cobra dumplings but not sure if they're on the menu at present. Happy eating.

🗩 **mickyw**

A couple of weeks ago Snakeboy (or something like that) was trying to find a restaurant serving snake. I'm very happy now that I may be able to help. On talking about it with my partner I was excited to discover that he knew where you can eat snake. It was about three years ago unfortunately but the place MIGHT still be open. He tells me it's on Bermondsey Street, where Snowsfields meets it on the opposite side of the road. It's 5 mins from London Bridge station.
He described it as far eastern/Balinese, can't remember the name, but they definitely had smoked cobra parcels along with other weird and wonderful things. Happy snake snacks.

🗩 **The Beak**

Pea

Is there anywhere in London that does a decent mushy pea fritter? I'm considering moving back to Devon simply because I can't find one here!

🗩 **Pelepeg**

Olleys in Herne Hill... gourmet fish and chips. Even my in-laws liked it! www.olleys.info/restaurant/holder.htm

🗩 **Gaijingirl**

Steak

I was in America recently (first time there, loved it!) and happened across the best ever steak of my life. *Ruth's Chris Steak House*, I shit you not, it is awesome. Anyway, I have now got a hankering for some really good dead cow. I can Google and read restaurant review websites with the best of them, but I'm after people's *personal* recommendations for the best steak in London. I don't mind paying handsomely for it, if it's worth it. I do mind paying handsomely for it if it's the same kind of yeh-not-too-bad-how-was-yours fare that you can get at most places. I'm looking for the BEST...

▭ **TheMoff**

TheMoff should get him/her self down to *The Gaucho Grill*; there are several of these divine Argentinean Steak Houses to choose from in our fine capital – The City, Canary Wharf, Chelsea and Mayfair. (I think there's one somewhere else too!) The steak is just *unbelievably* amazing... be warned it's not cheap though but it's worth it! You can find details of all of them on www.squaremeal.com. Enjoy!

▭ **Blonde Chick**

Best steak in London has to be *Pope's Eye Steak House*, 108 Blythe Road, W14 0HD. It follows the KISS principle (Keep it Simple Stupid) and only has steak on the menu, with many different sizes of course. It's a hard formula to stuff up, if you don't try to be too many things to too many people. So the only thing on the menu apart from steak, are side salads and fries that's it! Well, apart from the great wine list as well, to help those juicy morsels slide down... yum yum.

☐ snowjack

The best one I've had for a long long time was at *Smiths of Smithfields (SOS) Top Floor* restaurant. It came at a hefty price but I'm gonna remember it for some time! It was a special order for two people and you get about eight steaks off the bone with huge chunky chips, garlic butter, béarnaise sauce etc. It cost about £65 (for two) but boy was it worth it...

☐ The Pesk

I have to say the best steak I have ever had (and I've had a few) is at a restaurant called *The Old Etonian*, near the school at Harrow on the Hill (not strictly London I know). The starter and dessert is very average, but the fat fillet steak just melts in your mouth.

☐ moomee

The best steak in London? I am actually a bit loath to tell you this, or at least tell the rest of the world as it seems to be a reasonably well kept secret but... the place you want to go to is *The Guinea* on Bruton Place, w1. At the front it is a decent London boozer, popular with the local work crowd. At the back is the *Guinea Grill*, which, whilst not overly cheap, serves some of the best food in London. Not only are the steaks amongst the best I have ever had but if you like steak and kidney pies they have won the Steak & Kidney Pie Championship of Britain three times. Add to all this a great wine list and you have an evening very well spent.

☐ thecustardmonkey

The best steak I've had in London to date is from a fab restaurant called *Lightship X* in St Katharine's Dock. Not only does it serve ace food, it's also the oldest surviving lightship in Europe (or something like that) and a very unusual place to go for a romantic meal. Alternatively, my second best steak in London was one I bought from *M. Moen & Son* butchers on The Pavement near Clapham Common tube. Cook it on a griddle pan and you're done!

⌐ **Moomintroll**

I too am a lover of good, juicy steaks and the best I have found is at *La Pampa Grill* on Battersea Rise. It's an Argentinian place where the steak is served with fried eggs on top and garlic fries, mmm! The quality of the meat is superb, they don't overcook it like some places and if you go on a Friday or Saturday night, the waiters will usually oblige with some Argentine singing into the bargain.

⌐ **jerseygirl**

Sausage

Having worked exhaustively to discover every decent sausage roll outlet from Vauxhall to Victoria, I now have a new job and am struggling to find a decent one anywhere near Chancery Lane/Farringdon tube stations. Just a simple, honest sausage roll that hasn't gone sweaty in a glass display cabinet. Please can anyone help me?

⌐ **Woodster**

You need to walk a few minutes up Gray's Inn Road from where you are and head for *Konditor and Cook*. I had a sausage roll there today and it was the business. They also do a nice line in shepherds pie if you really want to push the boat out at lunchtime.

💬 Highbury Gal

Being a connoisseur of sausage rolls myself I always have a hunt for the *West Cornwall Pasty* stalls that are dotted around London. There is one in Wimbledon and London Bridge but I'm not sure where else. Never slimy and always nice Lincolnshire sausage. They rock my pastry world! *Greggs* aren't bad if you're in a fix, but once you go to *West Cornwall Pasty* you'll never look back.

💬 Clefty

Blood pudding

Internet searches fell at the first hurdle and I have just about reached the end of my tether. I need London's finest black pudding and I need it now. South-west London has proved a washout. Please any help anyone can give me would be most gratefully received. It might sound like a trivial request but it may just win me the hand of the woman I love.

💬 Delvin

Stornoway black pudding is supposedly up there with the best, although it tastes much like every other black pudding I've ever tried: www.wjmacdonald.com.

💬 Suckmonster

An alternative option is to take the object of your affections out to *Rules*, supposedly the oldest continually running restaurant in London, for their amazing quail's egg and black pudding salad starter. It goes nicely with a quarter bottle of shampoo, it has worked for me in the past! *Rules* is in Covent Garden and a bit pricey but very good value for what it is.

🗨 **leapy**

The best selection of excellent black puddings in London can be found in my opinion at the Borough Market, SE1, open Fridays and Saturdays. The *Sillfield Farm* stand has about four different varieties (plus white pudding) and there is a *Scottish Highland Beef* trader on the north side who does a sideline in black pudding and has just won yet another award for his version. As usual for Borough Market you won't be paying bargain prices but the quality is always very good and you know where your food comes from. Enjoy your puddings, I certainly have done!

🗨 **katjajulia**

Delvin! I would seriously reconsider my affection, if the mutuality of it depends on black pudding. Jeeez, you know what that stuff is made of? Brrrrr.

🗨 **ede**

Glass

Where have all the wonderful printed/moulded pint glasses gone? I miss looking down and being reminded what beer I'm drinking. They don't seem as common anymore. Neither do coasters for that matter. Has anyone else noticed this?

🗨 **Curry Monster**

In answer to Curry Monster's question, I don't know if this is right but I did a photoshoot for a drinks company last year and the bottles of Becks beer we were given were actually plastic. They looked exactly like glass bottles but were actually plastic and a bit lighter. We were told this is because all glass props in pubs and bars are being phased out. This is due to violent incidents. So we shouldn't hear about people being glassed in the face etc.

💬 reggae riot

Kebab

I've just returned from my third trip to Berlin and keep meaning to ask this – I was amazed when I first went there to be told that people eat kebabs in Berlin without being (a) drunk or (b) force-fed them. And when I tried one, they were absolutely wonderful, nothing like the 3am kebab I've on occasion woken up next to on a Saturday or Sunday morning in London after a big night out. So does anyone know where I can get a genuinely *good* kebab, i.e. one in proper flatbread and not too greasy that you can even have it for lunch?

💬 Juicy

Bosphorus (59 Old Brompton Rd, opposite Harts, SW7 3JS; 020 7584 4048). A Howler discovery, open until midnight seven days, serving very good Turkish grill items (7 days) in a hole-in-wall with extremely friendly service. Caution: prices are not as low as you'd expect, especially considering that you'll be leaning on counters or squatting on little

stools. But it's a good place to know about; their lamb
steak is a fine introduction to the superiority of British
lamb, chicken kebab is quite moist, with good grill flavour.
I uncharacteristically failed to try their bursa kebab
(aka Iskendar kebab, a bomb of a dish and one of my
all-time faves consisting of chunks of doner, butter croutons,
and yoghurt and tomato sauces). Nice fresh ingredients,
very reliable and super-friendly.

   Note: they have, according to their hypereccentric takeout
menu, 'gone as far as to test in a Scientific Laboratory for
fat content'. Chicken is 4.1%, shish is 5.6%, doner (same as
gyro or shwarma) is the fattiest at a whopping 23.5%.

💬 **peshman**

Flaming Nora's on Upper Street, Islington: www.flamingnora.com.
They're planning several more across London over the coming
months. Good burgers too, and they sell condoms and shower
gel in case you've just pulled.

💬 **londonplayboy**

Thanks both of you, I'll make sure I try them out soon! I don't
think I'd be stopping at a kebab shop if I'd pulled though.

💬 **Juicy**

Anatolya on Mare Street, Hackney E8. Friendly people
(they always offer me free Turkish tea while I'm waiting for
a takeaway). All food cooked on a traditional open charcoal
grill just a few feet from your table. They are licensed to sell
booze and serve reasonably priced meals with changing daily
specials. Recommended. ****

💬 **olly**

Efes, on Great Portland Street – can't recommend it highly enough. It definitely qualifies as a kebab to eat whilst sober. There's a takeaway next to the restaurant, never been to the restaurant though. Take out prices are very reasonable for the quality of food you get, it's about £4.50 for the most amazing shish kofte. It's about halfway down between Great Portland Street tube and Oxford Street: www.londontown.com/LondonInformation/Restaurant/Efes/7dce/.

💬 themoff

Seriously, how can you discuss good kebabs in London without mentioning Green Lanes or Dalston? Both are replete with the best, and cheapest, kebab restaurants outside Turkey. You really won't be disappointed.

💬 jeane

There's a place called *Tava* on Kingsland High Street about 5 mins north of Dalston Kingsland Station (big orange sign, on the left). This place is a decent Turkish restaurant but you won't pay more than £6 for a full meal. No spinning synthetic meat substitute here, it's all grilled over charcoal. There's little English spoken, which just adds to the charm for me. A bit further up Kingsland High Street there's a place called *Best Kebab*. I know it sounds awful, but bear with me... this is your genuine English adaptation of the kebab restaurant taken to as classy a level as possible; spinning horses' willies all over the place, but (as far as possible) the food is of a high standard, everything is fresh and they do all the trimmings.

💬 Twiglet

I've only ever eaten one kebab and it tasted like sweaty armpit smells. Then I did some work in Vatan's in Tottenham Hale, where they make the damned things (the ones that have bits sliced off while going round in front of a grill for days until there's toadstools growing out of it) and I still feel sick just thinking about it.

⌐ **Frank**

Everywhere else by London

Switzerland

Having just come back from a FANTASTIC holiday in the snow in Andorra, and feeling truly rotten to be back at work, my thoughts turn to food. After a gruelling day on the slopes there was nothing like stuffing myself silly with fantastic fondue, so I'm wondering, is there anywhere in London I can get a fondue?? Cheesy or meaty, I'm easy, I just want to pretend I'm back on hols! If there is I might even paint on a big red nose and give myself panda eyes to be authentic!

⌐ **Fabsal**

There is a Swiss restaurant in Soho that my friends and I went to as an Andorra ski-reunion night *St Moritz Restaurant*, 161 Wardour Street. The fondue was great, as was the raclette if I recall, but the rest wasn't up to much.

⌐ **Cheesemeister**

For the cheesiest fondue around, try *Tiroler Hut*, Westbourne Grove. Dining experience comes complete with piano accordion and live cowbell show.

💭 Boozehound

Mexico

I'm in search of some decent Mexican cuisine in London, and I'm hoping some LbLers will be able to help me with my quest. In the US you can find little tacquerias and takeout places everywhere, but they're fairly thin on the ground.

So far I've tried the (passable) *Texas Embassy* in Trafalgar Sq, the (fairly good) La Perla in Maiden Lane, very good takeaway from *The Cool Chile Co* in Borough, and a selection of god-awful tourist joints in Leicester Square, Greenwich and East Dulwich. There *must* be somewhere I can get freshly prepared, reasonably authentic and reasonably priced burritos, empanadas and margaritas in London! Elephant & Castle, where I live, has a thriving Latin community, but so far its only food outlet appears to be nachos at the *Wetherspoons*! Help, someone?

💭 babybat

The best Mexican food I have ever had in London was in Spitalfields market at lunch time. They have a variety of food stalls and restaurants serving every kind of food you might want. Some of them will give you tummy ache but the Mexican food stand always seems fresh, extremely tasty, fairly cheap and is fast. You can take away or eat on a picnic bench and watch the buskers perform. *Muy bien*.

💭 Hungry

I don't know if it's 'authentic' exactly, but the food at *Café Pacifico* on Langley Street, Covent Garden, used to be magnificent. The margaritas were good too, and they have a large selection of tequilas on the menu. I haven't been for years because it's always bombed, which is a good sign, I guess, if you can cope with crowds. I don't think they take reservations at the weekend, so you have to turn up early or take your chances at the bar.

🗨 **fluffy mark**

There is a lovely little Mexican place on Blackstock Road, in Finsbury Park called *Exquisite*. I haven't been there for a while but they used to do bargain deals on Sunday something like two dishes for a fiver. They also used to have a mad Russian waitress who mixed the best pitchers of Long Island Ice Tea I've ever had.

🗨 **Clefty**

You could do worse than the *Hobgoblin* pub in Brixton. Straight up Effra Road from the tube. They've been doing Mexican for a month or so now and the chef is the type of overenthusiastic Mexican food junkie that you want making your burrito rather than microwave boy. The setting in a pub is rough and ready but nothing comes to more than about £7 and I've never liked Mexican until now mainly through having been to crap Mexican chains etc. before.

🗨 **Mr Ben**

Ethiopia, via Vietnam

What with Chinese New Year having just passed (year of the rooster, cluck) my stomach started thinking of the Orient. I've had enough of Chinese food loaded up with MSG and wondered whether any of the LbL foodies could recommend a decent Vietnamese restaurant in this old town? Eagerly anticipating a break from the chicken and cashew nut norm.

💬 **BC The (Takeaway) Geek**

The best Vietnamese restaurant is the *Hanoi Cafe* on Kingsland Road. I've been to most of them round there and it's the only one that I have never had a bad meal from.

💬 **danny boy**

The *Vietnamese Canteen (An-Viet)* on Englefield Road has fantastic food, is cheap as chips and you can do BYO if you fancy. Try the tilapia in claypot, it's melt-in-the-mouth lovely.

💬 **pockettiger**

Song Que, 134 Kingsland Road, E2 is amazing – fab food, friendly staff, and wow how cheap. Apparently very authentic as well. Spring rolls will convert you from Chinese for good. A foodie query of my own; at work we've set up a lunch club where we visit a different country (by way of restaurant cuisine) each month have tried Peruvian, Spanish, American, Indian, Italian, North African, Vietnamese, Greek, Chinese, Irish, Thai and English (good old pie and mash) any suggestions for (unusual) others? Must be good value and within easy travelling distance of City. *Square Meal/London Eating* etc. can only give so much guidance.

💬 **Viet-Knatt**

How about Eritrean or Ethiopian? Try *Adulis*, 4446 Brixton Road, London, SW9 6BT, 020 7587 0055. Near Oval tube. Nice.

🗨 **Roger**

Ethiopian food – be warned, I think it tastes like fire wrapped up in mouldy bandages. You get this huge spongy white disc and you rip lengths of it off and wrap up the other stuff in it, which is tasty but very spicy, but the bandage-like stuff is made of half-fermented grain or something, and has a strange 'off'-tasting bitter taste, and feels slightly damp. Even the texture is bandagey, like those long crepe elasticated ones. Admittedly I didn't go to the one recommended in Oval... and I'm guessing it's an acquired taste which I'm not sophisticated enough to appreciate. However, instead, I recommend Gem, a Turkish restaurant, 265 Upper Street, N1. It's delicious.

🗨 **Albert**

I have to disagree with Albert – I thought Ethiopian cuisine was fantastic. The spongy pancake things are called injera and are a cross between a pancake and a crumpet. The meal I tried wasn't too hot, but a selection of vegetarian dishes that complimented each other. If you do try it, go for the coffee ceremony at the end, although you might not sleep that night... I think maybe you were just unlucky Albert.

🗨 **pockettiger**

Tapas

Having recently got back from a holiday in Spain where we devoured gorgeous tapas, we searched for a London restaurant offering the same this weekend. After looking on t'internet, we found that *Cafe*

Espania on Old Compton Street (no. 75) had many reviews claiming it to provide 'the best tapas in London'. We went to try it out, and must wholeheartedly (and belly-dly) recommend it to all. We had five tapas dishes (far too much), desert and a bottle of wine, and it came to £30. There's a huge menu, not just tapas, and it's a no-booking place, so you can just walk in or maybe wait 5 mins for a table. The staff were great and very polite, and full-on Spanish if you fancy a chat! Can't recommend it enough!

⌨ **Signorina**

I adore tapas and think I've now managed to get round every one, some of them not remotely authentic, in London. For the best tasting and best value, go to *La Vinas* in north London. It's on Whiteman Road in N4, right next door to Harringay station or a ten-minute walk from Finsbury or Manor House Tubes. For £35 you'll get a feast for two! It's closed Mondays.

⌨ **Chorizo Boy!**

Having lived in London for over eight years, and being half Spanish, I gotta say that I do miss good Spanish food, especially tapas. Place I can recommend is *Meson Don Felipe*, on The Cut. It's opposite the *New Vic*. The food is great, the service is great and every now and again you'll get some guy with a bright red shirt give the punters a Sevillana or two! *Olé!*

⌨ **El Guitarro**

I have been to many tapas bars in London – have still not found anything tastier or authentic than *Laxeiro* on Columbia Road, E2. The atmosphere is great and the food outstanding; only problem is that it gets very busy so need to book.

⌨ **Food Fan**

Not necessarily the best food, but the most 'authentic' tapas bar I have come across in London is the *Metro* inside Hammersmith tube station (HamCity station). Does really feel like one of the manic ones in Madrid or something.

☐ **Jase**

Talking of great tapas, I've just discovered a fab new deli in Shoreditch where they actually know how to keep cheese properly. A rarity in delis these days I find. Really enthusiastic, friendly staff (including a gorgeous girl in the cheese room, but I think she's married), and a great range of other food inc. fresh meat, wine, coffee, even flowers. Plus you can sit and eat it all on the premises. It's called *Food Hall Shoreditch*, next to the old Shoreditch Town Hall on Old Street. It's quite expensive, but worth every penny. Enjoy!

☐ **cheesy rider**

I went to *Cafe Espania* on a whim due to your suggestion. It was great. Super-fast service (although slightly agitated waiter) and cheap. Our grub was on the table seemingly before I'd even finished ordering it. Wholeheartedly recommended.

☐ **Satiated**

Another great venue for tapas is *Navarro's* on Charlotte Street. Lovely venue, with lots of wrought iron and painted tiling on the walls. Excellent menu, varied and plentiful. Is also very very good value for money. It's always busy which is testament to its popularity. We always go there for work dos even though it's a bit of a walk. On busy evenings the service can be a bit haphazard, but the food is so good I never really care.

☐ **classybird**

Salvador & Amanda's on Great Newport Street just behind Leicester Sq is the best place I've been to for tapas in ages. I've only been during the week, when it was fairly quiet, but have been told the atmosphere shouts out 'si senor' of a weekend. Sangria cocktails were great, and my favourite dish? Monkfish kebabs. Worst tapas I've had (please avoid) were at *Barcelona* on Wentworth Street (that's Petticoat Lane Market to those without East End knowledge). Arrived one Monday lunchtime, to find food being heated up from the previous Friday – grim!

💬 **Bruce**

One of the best places I've found is *El Rincon* on Clapham Manor Street in (surprise, surprise) Clapham. Good quality fresh food and very reasonably priced, and as some of the staff are Columbian some of the food is not your usual Spanish fare.

💬 **Willy**

I reckon the best I've tried anywhere in the UK in Mason Don Phillipe, in The Cut, opposite the Young Vic in Waterloo. It's been there for at least 15 years, well before tapas ever got trendy. Food is fabuloso. Staff are Spanish, and most evenings you get a guy (Rudolf Nureyev's younger, Spanish brother I reckon) playing real flamenco, without the tacky tourist drama, sitting on a little box balanced on top of the already crowded bar.

💬 **Mr Sniffy**

Hispanophilia

After years of travelling through Hammersmith's
H&C line station on the way to and from work,
I've recently discovered that *El Metro*, the rather
shabby-looking bar within the station concourse,
is actually very good. In fact, I'd go as far as to say
that it's the closest thing I've found to a genuine
Spanish tapas place in this lovely city (and I used
to live in Seville, so I know my cebollas, so to
speak). Azulejos on the walls, decent Spanish beer
and wine (not just San Miguel) and run by friendly
Spanish people – the food is decent and fairly
priced, and they'll even serve your tapas the proper
way if you want them like that (i.e. a beer, a little
munch, another beer, another little munch), rather
than forcing you to order everything at once, like
curry dishes. Anyway, a happy haven for hopeless
hispanophiles in happening Hammersmith.
Just thought someone might like to know...

💬 Juan Tan O'Mera

El Metro truly is a Spanish haven. In fact you'd have
to travel as far as Croatia to find a place like that
because the owner is in fact Croatian. As Spanish
as *O'Neills* is Irish. However, I have enjoyed many
a night in there mainly due to the fact that our office
is 90% female and they had a habit of playing
'pass the ice-cube'. Much to the frustration and
bemusement of the regulars who wanted to join in.

💬 Envman

Poland

I know there are a few Polish restaurants out Hammersmith way, but I haven't found any delis out there that will sell half-decent (not made in Wembley, frozen and shipped down) perogies (or piergies, if you prefer). There is a very nice Polish deli next to Streatham Hill station that sells wonderful perogies at a very reasonable price (£2/doz.), but it's really out-of-the-way for me. Does anyone know of a good Polish or Ukrainian deli that sells perogies elsewhere in the city? Best if they're home-made, but I've had some good stuff shipped over from Poland before. Decent kielbasa is a definite plus, but that's somewhat easier to find.

⌐ Chz

There is a Polish deli at the top of Latchmere Road, junction with Lavender Hill. Can't vouch for its quality but try it and see.

⌐ druster

What are perogies? There's a Polish deli very near me (Hammersmith way) and I've always wanted to go in and test out the Polish cuisine, but have held back 'cos I don't know what anything is and don't want to look silly! Maybe this is a delicacy I should be trying? Tell us what it is (and how to pronounce it) and you could be opening up a whole new world of food to me, and all those other LbLers! What a service!

⌐ Fabsal

Ethnia

Anyone know of any good and fairly genuine ethnic-type restaurants or eateries? I'm obviously discounting the Indian and Chinese places that I'm sick of (and should probably discount all Italian, French and Spanish places unless they are particularly cheap or interesting). Somewhere preferably fairly cheap, feels genuine (whether it is or not), and serves food from somewhere interesting. I guess I'd also like it to be kind of homely. Like those little places you pop into when you're abroad. I did hear of an Armenian restaurant out West ways, but promptly forgot where it was.

🗩 'Foreign Muck' Guy

I once took my girlfriend to a meal at *Souk 27* Litchfield Street. Unfortunately only a set menu was available and as my girlfriend is a vegetarian this was not ideal. However, the food was gorgeous (North African) and despite the set menu problem there was more than enough veggie things to make her happy. We went downstairs where the low ceilings and darkness made it superbly atmospheric. And you get to have a go at the strange Moroccan type pipe thingy afterwards too.

🗩 Food Man

There is a Brazilian restaurant on Richmond Way, w14 that is supposed to be the most authentic in London (but is there much competition out there?).

🗩 pippart

Ethnic food? Ooooh I love all that, me. For Greek, head
to Wood Green. *Vrisaki* on Myddleton Road is particularly
good. For Turkish, head to Dalston. *Mangal Ocakbasi*
on Arcola Street is particularly good. For Pakistani, head to
Whitechapel. *Lahore Kebab House* on Umberston Street
is particularly good. All very cheap, all miles from any tube
station, all full of relevant 'ethnics', all exceptionally good.

💬 **ed~money**

I went to a fab Georgian restaurant (Georgia the former
Russian state not the US one) in Hackney called *Little
Georgia*. Great food, lovely service and the Georgian wine is
pretty good too. Also there is a Sudanese restaurant in
Notting Hill that is super cool. Can't remember the name but
how many can there be? My friends and I make a point to
have dinner once a month. Someone gets to choose where
we go each month, it just has to be a different nationality
every time. We've been to some really cool places, and
haven't had a bad experience yet.

💬 **Food lover**

Here's one of the 'I love this secretish little place and
am loathed to make it less secret but hope others do the
same' tips. The *C&R* restaurant down the alleyway by *Pizza
Express* at the end of Gerrard Street in Chinatown is the
best eatery I've been to in London, and it's ethnic. It's got
less shabby in the last three years but the prices and
authentic Malaysian cuisine (I'm told by people who've
been there) has remained top notch (nasi goreng like a
Malay TV dinner is my usual). The owner and his family are
friendly and fast and if I tell them I did this maybe I'll get
a crazy seaweed sorbet thrown in next time I pop in.

It's a shining star in Chinatown, particularly now the *Dive Bar* has gone – anyone any joy on a suitably seedy substitute by the way?

💬 **Dave**

Scotland

As a Scot I occasionally hanker for the food of my home country. Does anyone know if there are any Scottish bakers, butchers or fish & chip shops in London? I miss butteries (rowies, morning rolls, call 'em what you will), macaroni pies, haggis suppers etc. I've made my own butteries, but who can be arsed with baking every Sunday morning? My Dad did tell me he found a bakers on Baker Street (how appropriate) that sold proper Scottish pies, but I've never been able to find it. And there's no way I'm buying a deep fat fryer for making proper chip-shop haggis suppers...

I know it's a long shot as there doesn't seem to be a proper Scottish community in London, but does anyone know of such places?

💬 **Muz**

Although a Sassenach, I lived in Scotland for five years and also sometimes have a hankering for the artery-filling treats of the auld country. I have been unsuccessful in finding a true Scottish-style chippie (particularly the really handy ones that sell juice, fags, coffee, washing powder etc. until four in the morning), London appearing to be too addicted to fried chicken and kebabs, and hampered by licensing laws, to have them. However, I have discovered that by bizarre colonial coincidence a close variant of the macaroni pie is also a culinary delicacy of Trinidad and Tobago; there are a few Trinidadian shops in Lambeth that sell it, the best in my opinion being *Roti Joupa* on Clapham High Street by Clapham North tube.

꒰ **Tree**

My Glaswegian friend tells me you can buy butteries in Harrods.

꒰ **Sassenach**

Since there's been a few Scots posting in the last few weeks and upholding stereotypes by discussing pies and booze etc. this may be of interest. There's a quarterly drinks night called (imaginatively) 'Scots' in London held at the *Royal Scottish Corporation* in Covent Garden. It sounds stuffy and it started off as a bit of an excuse for public school City types to get blootered together but that's all changed now due to infiltration by random (Scottish) punters such as myself, a group from the London arm of the Tartan Army, SNP etc. Trust me, it's a good night of boozing, meeting fellow Scots, networking if you want and more boozing.

   The more quality people that come along the better it'll get. And the best bit is you pay £10, which goes to charity and that's all your food and drink paid for the rest of the night. Result. Last time there was a funny drunk lady. Someone there is bound to know where you can get a haggis supper in London etc. Next one is not till January, details here: www.royalhigh.org.uk/rhsevents.htm#drinks.

꒰ **The Assassin Prince**

Liber-tea

I don't know if anyone else ever feels that sometimes one just wants to sit shivering the alcohol out of one's bloodstream in an more rarefied atmosphere than that of the greasy spoon on Stroud Green Road? *Liberty* is not only the most drool-inducing department store, but their cafe has simply bucketloads of rarefied atmosphere, and the most adorable mishmash of little chairs and big chairs and tables and pretty pictures on the walls. Their scones are heavenly and come with three little bowls of jam and they have cakes and coffee too, of course, and quite frankly I cannot think of a nicer place to take tea.

💬 Mr Sandling

Holland

Some Dutch family members are coming to visit soon, and we'd like to be able to provide them with an attempt at their favourite Dutch foods. Does anyone know a shop (or even better a cafe/restaurant) that sells stroopwaffels, vla, and their absolute favourite, poffertjes? Ideally West, but have an Oyster card and not afraid to use it.

💬 Daisy

The big *Londis* on the corner just before the *Adelaide* pub on Adelaide Road (near Chalk Farm) sells stroopwaffels. You can also get fake ones in most *Starbucks*. Yum!

💬 mindy manilow

My Old Dutch on High Holborn is a Dutch pancake house. No idea how authentic it is, but there you go.

🗨 **jonno**

I'm not aware of a shop as such. If someone comes back with details of one, my diet is about to go out of the window! But *De Hems* Dutch bar on Macclesfield Street by Chinatown (www.dehems.co.uk) serves all the right hot Dutch snacks – bitterballen, kaasouffles, frikandellen etc. Very good beers, Dutch TV, footie games... it has the lot. By the way, *Starbucks* sell something very similar to stroopwaffels but unfortunately not quite so gooey!

🗨 **Ali**

The sub-continent

Since I subscribed to LbL about two years ago I have started doing far more interesting things in London than ever before, and am full of interesting/annoying titbits of information about the place that I thrill all my friends with. However, there is one major thing that I still haven't done and that is have a curry in Brick Lane. I really want to go but was just wondering if there are any restaurants I definitely have to try or definitely should strike off the list. Any ideas?

🗨 **Polly**

Aladin. Definitely *Aladin*. It's just the best 'proper' curry, not pricey in the least and simply gorgeous food. Bring your own wine and do NOT ask them to play that bloody 'Prince Charles recommends' tape EVER!

🗨 **curry comber**

Having used to live on Brick Lane for three years, me and my flatmates were frequent visitors of the numerous curry houses. They're all pretty good; however, I'd probably say *Bengal Village* or *Preem* were the best ones. They're both opposite each other.

However, avoid the likes of *Cafe Naz* though!

💬 **Hong Kong Suey**

Do not under any circumstances go to *Nazrul;* this is absolutely the worst curry I have had in my entire life dodgy-tasting mint yoghurt, dubious chicken and the strangest-tasting peshwari naan ever plus the service was awful. Instead go to the *Monsoon;* have had several lovely evenings in there now, and it's usually packed out.

💬 **Chris**

Quick tips re Brick lane: (1) avoid any curry house with a fellow outside offering a good deal etc. First and last time I was sucked in the samosas were insufficiently, er, microwaved and we walked out. The fellow did not honour his promise to refund if not fully satisfied. (2) Go to *Aladin*. It's not glamorous and you must take your own booze, but it's cheap, the food is good, there's no slick patter AND if you ask nicely they will play you their tape of HRH Prince Charles endorsing the very place you are sitting. Priceless. (Or if not priceless can anyone get me a price for having Prince Charles endorse me?) Just remember to applaud.

💬 **magpiepokinggeezer**

I live and work near Brick Lane and have had many a curry, none of them bad. What you have to realise about Brick Lane before you go however, is that it is really catering for the English market; this is Angla-Bangla at its best, with things like korma, rogan josh and madras on the bestsellers list. If you're looking for really good, authentic Indian food, then the only place to be is *New Tayyabs* on Fieldgate Street, not far away. It's cheap, busy and really, really good but there's not a tikka in sight. But if it's Brick Lane you're after, you can't go wrong with *Bengal Cuisine*, *Bengal Village*, *City Spice*, *Nazrul* (bad decor, good food) or my personal favourite *Cafe Naz*. If you're lucky, they'll be playing Bollywood movies on the big screen.

Actually, while I'm at it, I'm going to share a secret; just off Brick Lane on Heneage Street, is a little pub called *Pride of Spitalfields*. It's a proper East End boozer, with friendly folks, nice prices, and crucially it seems to always still be open well past 11pm.

💬 Little G

Pastries and pasties by London

Pastries

Can anyone recommend a good Italian bakery especially one with fresh pastries? After much searching, I've come up empty and am hoping that the wisdom of my fellow LbLers will come to the rescue. Thanks so much.

💬 Paperboat

I don't think that they actually do the baking but *Bar Italia* off Old Compton Street does some pretty good Italian pastries. *Belissima! Amalfi* is a good pastry shop run by Italians on Old Compton Street. *Bellisimisimisima!* Good coffees too!

💬 mappeal

I know what you mean. Try a place on the Kings Road called *Made in Italy*. It's run by a gang of young Italians. They do things like little puff pastry horns filled with lemon ricotta and exceptional rum babas. The Proper Deal and nothing like the load of mediocre old crap that often passes for Italian food in this country.

☐ **Justonecornetto**

Pasties

I just spent the hottest weekend of the year serving up lashings of lumpy bum gravy to my toilet, desperately trying to stem the flow with Immodium, which is bad for you, I am told by all and sundry. This is the third time in about nine months that I have been food poisoned and the thing I hate the most about it is that I cannot get the culprits back, because I have eaten the evidence. Henry VIII had the right idea in that he used to boil poisoners alive (I think, though I can't be arsed to check and perhaps this could start another thread if I am talking rubbish anyway).

However, assuming the evil libel lawyers don't bring down LbL, I think it would be a good idea to name and shame them. So I shall begin with the ham and cheese pie from the *Gregg's* off Golden Square in Soho, although I probably deserved this one, and the beef and ale pie from the *Glassblower* on Glasshouse Street in Soho. And to add insult to injury there were about two pieces of cartilaginous beef in it. I can't remember the third one. Maybe I should stop eating pies.

☐ **Fleance**

Oh, Fleance. How can you say such terrible things about *Gregg's*, esteemed purveyors of the finest pastry and Mechanically Recovered Meat products in town? Their sausage rolls, their pies, their slices, you name it, are all delectable. Hell, even their donuts (although not much meat in them. Well, some, probably)... Perhaps you hadn't washed your hands properly that day? I, for one, am off to get a two for £1.10 deal on their sausage rolls immediately. What are everyone else's favourite mystery meat slurry and pastry products? Personally, I think scotch eggs have got to be the ultimate. And, with new 'party' size, you can now snack on them all day.

⌨ Tiddles

London by boozer

Pubs

Now, on the subject of pubs. There are two issues at stake here to rescue me from yet another winter of fruitless tramping about. I want:
a) cosy pubs in central London with dartboards;
b) pubs in London that serve BAR sausages. Not with loads of mash and gravy and stuff, just on their own, with a little pot of mustard. Mmmmm. No greater pub snack – beats crisps and pork scratchings any day. Anyone have a clue? There's the *Windsor Castle* in Notting Hill, but that's it for my knowledge...

⌨ Stella Rimington

A bowl of hot sausages usually sits in a corner of the bar at *The Grenadier*, a tiny pub tucked between Knightsbridge and Belgrave Square, at the centre of a labyrinth of alleys. Often fills up at rush hour with American tourists and hooray pinstripes but is well worth a look-in, particularly for a quiet afternoon pint at the weekend.

💬 dalziel

As for Stella Rimington's request for pubs with dartboards. A former ageing work colleague of mine would always gravitate to *The Angel* on St Giles High Street, because '...it's the only bloody pub in the centre of London with a dartboard.' I'm not saying he's infallible, but, believe me, he knew his pubs. I have a feeling that the dartboard is becoming an endangered species in London, though.

💬 robram

Drink

Well done to London Underground who have now installed a refreshments (coke, diet coke and H_2O) dispenser/vending machine at Stockwell (on the southbound Northern line). Or should we thank Cadbury's, the supplier of the chocolate vending machines for taking the initiative to listen to the Underground travellers who wrote into them with requests to supply liquids rather than chocolate? Let's hope more pop up on the Underground!

💬 Wiesiee

Greenery

Now that summer is here and my first in London I've been making a special effort to stay out of doors. The important thing however, is that this doesn't interfere with my drinking. I have decided that pubs with big gardens are the ideal solution. Unfortunately where I live (Elephant & Castle way) there is little in the way of actual greenery there are a few courtyards, but what I really need is some kind of alcohol-themed Narnia, where you step through the back door of the pub into a colossal green space, with grass and trees and tables and benches and maybe a little stream or a pond and some livestock. Anyone know of such a pub? Preferably Zones 13.

🗩 yuri

Not quite livestock, but I had a Narnia-type experience when I used to frequent the garden of Brixton's *Duke Of Edinburgh* on Ferndale Road a couple of years ago: www.urban75.org/ brixton/photos/178.html. Not the nicest pub inside, but it has a huge beer garden and they do (or at least did) big old bbqs during the summer. Yum. They also used to have a nice pet kitten (probably a cat now)... miaow.

🗩 **Brucey**

Yes, the 'Elph isn't great for outdoors boozing, but the *Beehive* in Carter Street is a charming pub with lots of tables outside on the concrete (there's a few hanging baskets and the like for colour). For full-on beer garden elysium, among the best Sarf Landan has to offer is the *Sun & Doves* in

Coldharbour Lane, Camberwell. The garden there is uncannily
close to your description of an 'alcohol-themed Narnia'.

💬 **ninorc**

Surely the answer to your plea for anyone in south London
has to be the *Windmill* on Clapham Common.

💬 **the elephant man**

Try the *White Horse* on the corner of Parsons Green.
Take the District line going towards Wimbledon and get off
at Parsons Green, turn right out of the station and walk
up towards the green, the pub is on the left-hand side,
about 30 yards, as you walk up. You can buy your drinks
and go and sit on the green, it's close enough to get back
to the bathroom too. It's also known as the 'Sloaney Pony'
by the locals and regulars.

💬 **peshman**

The *King's Arms* in Wandsworth, at 96 Wandsworth High
Street, they've got a massive beer garden with loads of grass
flowers, enchanting walls and bird baths etc. etc. and they're
in the process of building a patio area to put a pagoda on.
Bar staff are really friendly but be warned at lunch time on a
sunny day you have to get in early to get a seat outside!!

💬 **crofty**

Slightly closer than the 'Sloaney Pony' in Parsons Green as
suggested by Peshman is *The Duke of Devonshire* in Balham.
The garden is not huge, but it definitely has most of the
Narnia features you're looking for. The pub is open late some
days of the week. Enjoy!

💬 **Friendly Geek**

Hack

 As one of a handful of journalists left on Fleet Street itself I'm quite interested in the history of the street and its links with my fine trade. I've read about a pub called 'The Stab in the Back'. But despite Googling, I can't find any info on it. Is it a legend? Does it still exist but has been renamed or something? Clearly I'm not an investigative journalist or I'd have been able to find out for myself.

 The Assassin Prince

The pub you're referring to was known by hacks as the 'Stab in the Back' it is the *White Hart* on New Fetter Lane – try it, if only for the newspaper memorabilia on the walls

 robram

London by locale

LBL greatest hits: it's a date

I'd very much like to have some suggestions for a restaurant that will fit these criteria:

1. Suitable for taking a girl on her birthday. Not too flashy but intimate without being overbearing I would say.
2. I am a struggling journo so £80–100 absolute tops, preferably even less without looking cheap, including a healthy alcohol quotient (I never trust newspaper

reviews where they seem to manage on one half
bottle between five when totting up prices).

3. Cuisine is fairly open but maybe along the lines of
seafood. Personally I like a good feed so none of that
nouvelle malarkey. Also, are all the lastminute.com-type
offers for cheap meals at The Ivy and so forth rubbish?
Someone must have tried them what's the catch?
Seats by the lavatory and bread and water only
or something?

💬 Laurence

I recommend *Vasco & Piero's* on Poland Street. Not too
expensive, great food, works a treat for dating.

💬 Ed

Oh God yes! I know where you could take her: *Andrew
Edmunds* on Lexington Street w1 (020 7437 5708). It's very
small and so definitely intimate. The tables and chairs are
rickety and non-matching – this isn't particularly a selling
point, they just are. Dribbly candles cast very flattering
lighting (she'll appreciate that) and the food is divine.
The menu changes weekly and is handwritten a nice touch.
The staff are jolly helpful and will help you chose the perfect
wine to suit you (unlike the waiters in *Quo Vadis* who
serenely glide around on their oiled casters intimidating
diners into ordering fantastically expensive wines I pointed
at a £25 bottle of wine to which the oily one tutt tutted and
said he thought my guest boyfriend of yonks thank God and
so not needing to be impressed would prefer this one and
pointed to a £70 bottle! A pox on him).

Anyway, I can't remember what I ate, I just remember
loving it *Andrew Edmunds* that is. Four of us went and had

starters and mains and the boys had puddings (don't
they always?) and a bottle of fizz to begin with and then
a shed-load of red. The bill was £50 each. If you're taking
a young lady out you probably don't want to follow our
lead on the amount drunk. As I said, I don't remember what
I ate... Good luck.

💬 **Hels**

Andrew Edmunds on Lexington Street is a lovely, reasonably
priced romantic restaurant. If you want intimate, you will get
it here. The seating plan is cosy, food is hearty and tasty,
wine list is good and priced across a range. Service is
friendly. You might even forget you are in w1.

💬 **Ang**

I'd recommend two things in terms of food in London.
One is www.toptable.co.uk – it's great to get ideas and
registering often allows you special discounts and offers for
food at some of the best restaurants in London. My choice
for a 'top table' though, would be *Le Boudin Blanc* in
Shepherds Market. The setting is great and the food French.
It's not crazily expensive for London (80 quid for two) but the
setting is fantastic. Quiet little market square with pubs all
around. Opposite Green Park, so nice for walking to after a
stroll in the park, and near the tube station.

💬 **Crazy Eddy**

I have a few suggestions for Laurence about where to take a
girl for her birthday. Not sure where you are based but here
are some places I'd like to be taken in similar circumstances:
• *Smiths of Smithfields*. The middle restaurant is lovely and
  not too expensive (compared to the top one). They have

a really good menu, including a good selection of meat
and fish in a really nice atmosphere. Small wooden
tables, low lighting but not too much of an intimate vibe.

- *The Rivington Bar and Grill*. Top food, good sized portions
  and a nice lounge area where you can sit and have
  another few bottles of wine after your meal. It's in the
  middle of Old Street and Great Eastern Street.
- *Cru*. Really great food, and very chilled, it's lit by tea
  lights but still has hustle and noise from the kitchen.
  It's near Hoxton Square.

There's also a really nice pub in Hammersmith called the
Anglers Arms that does the best pub grub ever and not only
that but they have tonnes of blackboards filled with every
choice of wine you could hope for and it's all at pub prices!
Hope that helps.

💬 **Pesk**

For moderately cheap and good you can't do better than
Upper Street. Three winners in terms of romantic but not
cheesy ambience and good portions are:

- *Le Mercury*. You could definitely do a good meal for
  two people for £70 here. Nice little French place,
  right near Almeida Theatre. Romantic ambience. Book in
  advance as it is popular.
- *Le Petit Auberge*. Over the road from Mercury. Fantastically
  interesting menu with game and exotic fish that changes
  all the time.
- *Casale Franco*. You have to keep your eyes open to
  spot this place the entrance is down a back alley next
  to *Vultures* video shop and it shares this entrance with
  a car mechanic's! However, don't let this less than
  glamorous first impression put you off. It is lovely

inside and the food is simply outstanding. When I went I had seafood risotto and it was cracking; wine was pretty good too.

Matthew

For fish I would definitely recommend *Livebait*. Me and my bloke had a romantic dinner there (at the Covent Garden one) to celebrate our anniversary and after three courses and a bottle of nice and not too cheap wine and coffees and stuff it came to £80. They source their fish ethically if you're into that sort of thing, and you can look at the amazing display they have near the kitchen. If you like shellfish they do this fantastic platter to share, with lobster and gigano prawns, and mussels, whelks, cockles all that kind of stuff. I had the most amazing melty halibut rarebit thing when we were there. They also have a pre-theatre menu which is a steal. The only downside for your evening of lurve is that it has a very (deliberate) canteen feel. The whole place is tiled which means when the place is full the chatter is very loud, and it's not lit particularly romantically. However, we unintentionally timed our meal from about 6.45pm until about 9pm, so the place really emptied out of the pre-theatre crowd and got quite mellow until the regular diners turned up as we were getting ready to leave. And they gave us a little table in the corner near the door which is sheltered by a partition thingy, so we did feel quite protected from the crowd. But the tables are quite packed in and it was pretty noisy in the busy periods, but the service was fine and the fish was fab. Anyway, not sure it fits all your criteria, but worth a look. Hope it helps, enjoy your dinner!

Sqweno

May I suggest *Julie's* in Notting Hill Gate? Fits all the specs
you're looking for and is absolutely magic! Call and reserve
a room in the 'Forge' (or the little room at the end of it and
to the left). Pictures, menus etc. are all available at their site:
www.juliesrestaurant.com. Good Luck.

💬 **Garth**

La Bouchon by South Kensington station is perfect.
Surprisingly cheery French hospitality, great wines, great food.
Tres, tres romantic. Bill for two with two bottles of wine and
two courses was about £75 when we went.

💬 **gizbourn**

Marine Ices in Chalk Farm Road – dead good Italian food;
three courses for less than 20 quid each without booze,
the ice cream menu is fantabulosa, take some home to bed!
And the staff are nice.

💬 **Maureen**

First date

I can see from the LbL FAQ that there has been a
long-running thread about great date restaurants,
but what about magical bars for a first date?
My specifications are quite strict: it should definitely
not be so outrageously noisy that you can't hear each
other talk... it should be fairly classy... and it should be
unusual/magical/special. *Loungelover* would be a good
example of what I'm thinking of, but more suggestions
would be great!

💬 **Harriet**

You should try the bar at *Claridges*. Yes, it's expensive, but the waiters are the best in London, the free bar snacks are to die for and it must be the classiest bar in London. Oh, and the drinks are pretty good too...

      💬 **Highbury Gal**

For a truly roasting first date there is a bar on Great Titchfield Street called *Firevault*. Don't be put off by the upper floor (a classy shop for fireplaces) head down the stairs and towards the back. There is a peaceful, very cool den of tables, intimate lighting and fabulous service. Would recommend it for a different/classy date.

      💬 **Penelope Pitstop**

Waterstones Piccadilly top-floor bar. Great views, decent cocktails (if a little pricey), makes you look impressively literate/London-knowledgeable that you know of this hidden bar, and is genuinely a nice place to go. Can be a bit smoky, and occasionally crowded, but is a good place to meet up.

      💬 **Scott**

Another fab date place is Vertigo 42. Up on the top floor of Tower 42 (old Nat West tower) in the City, this place simply oozes class. Panoramic views of London, wonderful cocktails and sophisticated snacks what more could you ask for? Reservations are a must, and being at the top of an office block there is tight security. More of a pre-dinner drink spot, could have dinner at *Rhodes Twenty Four* afterwards. Level 42, Tower 42, 25 Old Broad Street, London, EC2N 1HQ, www.vertigo42.co.uk.

      💬 **Paula**

Chips

I've got a massive chip on my shoulder about the middle classes... I realise that not all public-school educated people lack social skills (some of my best friends are middle-class) but those long vowels just do my head in. Anyhoo, how about a bit of public therapy? Some of you warm, friendly, well-mannered, helpful people must be middle-class so, if I just vent a tiny bit, maybe some of you can talk some sense into me? Nice one, here goes...

First up, all of you, stop shouting it's rude. Just because you've been bred to think you're better than everyone else doesn't mean you are. That arrogance of yours, that's just fear you'll be rumbled. And I don't care how much money you've got, what your dad does or what school you went to. What's the deal with your gene pool? You're all horsey-faced blondes, or six-foot, balding, thick browed clones stop marrying your cousins. Oi mate! Yes you, don't talk to women like that, it's not charming it's demeaning. Stop dressing like 'Father' and get some trousers that reach your brown deck shoes. In fact, ditch the deck shoes and stop tucking your shirt in at the weekend. Look love, yes you, stop rah-rah-rahing, calm down and use your normal voice you can still be strong, assertive, individual and independent without discarding your femininity and going all blokey. Lastly, rugby's rubbish and manners cost nothing.

Lovely. Cheers for that more of a bigoted rant than a vent. Right then, are all these defects down to public school and working for Foxton's or what?

Come on London... confirm or deny. And yes, I was bullied as a child. Derided as posh at school because we had four bedrooms (and a 'study'... la-de-da), and too sweary and good at football to be proper middle-class.

💬 calm as you like

I know that everyone is entitled to his or her own opinion but I think it's awful that LbL printed 'calm as you like's' response. You wouldn't print something overtly racist or sexist (I assume) so why print this? If I ever happened to meet 'calm as you like' I'd gladly punch him or her for being such a narrow-minded, arrogant moron. And shame on LbL for publishing the response.

💬 Lulu

Original

I have a friend who has been to every bar, eaten at every restaurant etc. Does anyone have any suggestions for somewhere original/sexy/weird/ underground/out of the way/bizarre/strange to take him for dinner/drinks on his birthday? I have run out of imagination but am sure there must be somewhere out there that will still surprise such a jaded Londonite. Any clubs/members' clubs where you just pay to join etc. would be interesting. All suggestions welcomed.

💬 East End Girl

How about the *Hat on Wall* if he's not been there? It's a bar on Hatton Wall (number 2428). It's not that easy to find and

you have to press a buzzer to get in, but it's great.
The people are a real mix. We went at about 7ish pretty
early and it was dead, but within about 45 minutes was
packed with all sorts. The staff were really friendly, there
were comfy seats, tasty cocktails and people were chatty
and friendly too. It wasn't pretentious at all either which
we were worried it had the potential to be when we went
in. Definitely worth a look though, I'd say. You have to be
careful though, because there are certain nights they aren't
open or they've got private parties on – it's worth calling to
check 020 7242 9939.

Nancy Drew

Somewhere I've always wanted to go to is *Milk and Honey*
on Poland Street. It is a members' club but if you phone in
advance you can get in, certainly on quieter days of the
week. It's styled on a New York 1920s prohibition-era
speakeasy (you have to buzz to get in) and is very dark
and atmposheric. Check out the website for details:
www.mlkhny.com.

Crouch Ender

Having to work near the City fairly regularly and fancying
a pint or two after work leaves you with the usual options
of paying an arm and a leg for piss poor warm beer,
sharing three centimetres of fake mahogany bar space
with a hoard of load wannabe-Sloanettes, Timnicebutdims,
bewildered Italian English language students looking for the
Tower, and worst of all, City types braying how clever they
are while secretly longing to work somewhere that involves
a little creativity and less selfishness. Soooo *The Cittie of York*
(crazy spelling, I know, but go with it) on High Holborn is

your friend, just opposite Chancery Lane tube. Run by an indie brewer (Samuel Smiths) it offers strange German lagers that taste like, well, lager, and have different strengths, cost just about two quid and there's a decent-sized hall/ roomy thing and private little alcoves off the main room for uninterrupted chats. Just don't all go and tell everyone!

💭 **Darling**

Music

Does anyone know a great place where you can have a fabulous meal and listen to live dinner music? Have been to *Ronnie Scott's, 606* **etc. but prefer something a bit more intimate with better food.**

💭 **Shazza**

Check out the *Troubadour* on the Old Brompton Rd, between Earls Court Road and Warwick Road, it's got a fab downstairs dinner/jazz/live band cellar. It's got a pretty intimate upstairs, looks a bit like a continental cafe... the food's generally top notch and affordable too.

💭 **Peshman**

Well, it's not *that* intimate however, it has excellent food and live music at the weekend – *MEZZO*! It's on Wardour Street... the 'proper' restaurant downstairs is the one with the live band... food is excellent, as is their cocktail list!

💭 **Blonde Chick**

And finally

Diet

I would like to consult a dietician/nutritionist (don't know the difference). I'm not really overweight and I don't have any real health problems but I feel I'm missing out on optimum health and energy. I've looked in the *Yellow Pages* but there is a huge array of ads and I have no idea what to go for and how much I should be paying. Can anyone help, preferably south of the river or central London?

⌐ **Health Freak**

Try *Neal's Yard* in Covent Garden; they offer a whole range of holistic therapies, including naturopathy, which (if you don't know) deals with nutrition amongst other things. I went a while ago for the same reason – nothing specific but not feeling 100% – and the lady I saw gave me lots of good advice on my diet, which did make a difference (until I started drinking again!!). And, all sessions are only £20 on a Saturday morning!

⌐ **Rainy Tuesday**

Entertainment

Ahh, London. The city that never sleeps. Well, alright then, the city that sleeps occasionally (perhaps some kind of power nap) then jumps out of bed and immediately gets on a horse; the city that enjoys a round of urban golf as much as a  game of beach volleyball; the city that likes to slip into its silky shorts for a quick slam dunk before relaxing with a spot of lunchtime yoga; the city that rushes across town to a poetry reading with its tap shoes still on its feet; the city that will make you laugh more than a Chinese Elvis. In short, if you can't find something to keep you entertained in London in the next few pages, then it's most probably time that your lifeless body was lowered into the unforgiving ground.

Lonely by London

Not getting any

I was looking at the pictures on the LbL site today – my we're a handsome bunch. I think you should organise an LbL speed-dating event so that we can breed and create an LbL master race of gorgeous beings with an above-average knowledge of London trivia. Also, I haven't been getting any recently. Did you guess?

🗨 **Will's sister**

I haven't been getting any recently either. If Will doesn't mind, maybe I could get it on with his sister. Our offspring would have an in-built guidance system to London's best boozers and a natural aversion to American tourists...

🗨 **Anna's brother**

I think it's a fine idea. Personally I'm looking for a speed dating event that isn't full of tragic figures working in recruitment or media sales. Maybe someone out there knows one?

🗨 **Mike**

Interesting to hear you're looking for a speed dating event that isn't full of tragic figures working in recruitment or media sales. Surely speed dating is the tragedy here. In our beautiful city full of exciting places, fabulous events and gorgeous women only social halfwits have to resort to speed dating. Come on Mike. Get your life together. This city is bursting with opportunities to meet amazing, clever, sexy women.

PS. I work in media sales. Have done for ages. How about a new strand of conversation about uncool London jobs that are actually cool? I propose media sales. Great money, the chance to work for amazing media brands and a great work/life balance.

💬 **Winnersandlosers**

Winnersandlosers, I think you've been a bit harsh on poor Mike. Speed dating isn't my idea of fun either. I'd rather swallow razor blades, but each to his own. I'm by no means a bog-monster, in fact, under the right light, I'm considered attractive, not to mention funny and intelligent (no lighting needed for the last two) but I do find it increasingly difficult to meet interesting *single*, straight men.

I work in the music industry, and work life sort of merges into social life without you even noticing (not a complaint, in fact, often a plus, I know I'm in a lucky position here) but it's a small industry, everyone knows everyone. So c'mon then, where are all these sexy (and more importantly) interesting, intelligent people? I assume if there are sexy smart women, their male counterparts have to be in the same place?

💬 **nowlookhereyoungman**

I have to take issue with the correspondent who thinks media sales is a 'cool' career. If responding to a colleague's shout of 'sold' by jumping on the desk and applauding is 'cool', then I'm a monkey's father's brother.

💬 **Peter**

With regard to meeting normal single blokes in London I too think it's really bloomin' tricky. In fact my friends who live in small country towns have far more flirtations than I have ever had in my five years in London (most of that time being single). I don't even have a high-powered job that I can blame it on. London is not an easy place to meet nice random people and all my other single London friends agree (both male and female). It's odd 'cos I see plenty of nice-looking blokes get on the trains every day, but where do they all go out?? Do they all stay in with their girlfriends, or do they all turn in to sweaty drunken nutters in the evening?

London should be a melting pot of exciting encounters, and in some respects it absolutely is, but in the boyfriend department, sadly not always the case.

But having fun anyway!

In response to But having fun anyway's comments about it being easier to meet people outside of London, I totally agree! I am a Londoner born and bred and love both living and working in London. However, meeting decent attractive guys seems to be really difficult even though I would say I have a great group of friends and a fun social life. My friends outside of London however seem to meet people much more regularly. What's a girl to do?

Single gal in London

Sordid

I can hold back no more. I'm in love! What's more, I'm in love with the sweetest, sexiest, least inhibited man I've ever met, and it's absolutely fantastic. All of my friends hate me because I'm just so deliriously happy all the time and now you hate me too. Ha! The reason I am writing, however, is to ask for your help in finding decent public places to make love in. So far our favourites have been underwater in

Hampstead pond and in the toilets of the *Tate Modern*. Does that sound sordid? It was. It was marvellous. We're going up the *London Eye* this weekend, but if anyone can give me a few more suggestions, that would be great. ;-)

␌ elena

The lavatories in the *National Gallery* are quite good for that sort of activity and although they are decidedly spooky, the toilets in *Just St. James* are good too (also get a good feed)! Although I would imagine you don't just want toilets, alas I'm yet to go truly al fresco in London!

␌ IrisRed

Dirty

I'm planning to take the wife to London for our first anniversary and need some ideas for must-see stuff to do and non-extortionate places to stay. I'm thinking nice spots on the river for a moonlit wander where I'm not going to get stabbed by a crack whore, little out of the way places that don't normally show up on the tourist radar and things that aren't full of pseudo middle-class ponces that cost the earth. Yes I've looked on Google, no I haven't seen anything that inspires me. Any suggestions of entertaining shows which don't require a degree in satirical literature would be greatly appreciated.

␌ I'd visit but I'd never live there

You are obviously a boring provincial with a chip on his shoulder and big city paranoia who is about to be roundly and justifiably flamed by LbLers, i.e. you and the wife would be better off just staying home.

🗨 **the errorist**

Any chance of telling the author of 'Dirty' not to bother visiting London? His condescending punch line (I'd visit but I'd never live there) and sad attempt to be cool and knowing (stabbed by crack-whores indeed) make me think that the brilliance of London (its people, buildings, cultures, bars, restaurants, history, night-life, art, creativity, energy etc.) is wasted on him. For a safe experience with the wife I suggest he never leaves home. Though beware crack-addicted burglars murdering innocent suburbanites for the price of a couple of rocks, mannnnnnnnnn.

🗨 **mickyw**

Alan Partridge's response: 'Go to London. I can guarantee you'll either be mugged or not appreciated.' You can walk by the river most places in London without being 'stabbed by a crack whore'. And if you want to watch a show 'which don't require a degree in satirical literature' then I imagine *Tonight's the Night: The Rod Stewart Musical* would fit the bill. It was written by Ben Elton you know.

🗨 **Laurence**

I can't wait for all the replies telling 'I'd visit but I'd never live there' that if he's too scared of the people in London, too tight to get his wallet out to celebrate his anniversary, and too devoid of imagination even with the help of Google, not to bother bringing his wife to London but to stay at home and get a video out instead. Happy anniversary, by the way.

🗨 **Crack Whore**

Lungsful by London

Smoke

Is there *anywhere* in London you can go see a film and have lovely fag at the same time? (Apart from my living room.) Got a friend who is a 60-a-day woman and can I get her to go to the cinema? Can I buggery – she reckons she can't do an hour without a fag. So are there any nicotine-friendly cinemas left in London? I'm after ones which show new releases, not the type where you would normally wear a dirty mac.

desperate smoker

The last I heard the *Coronet* in Notting Hill still allowed you to smoke. If you remember the 'hilarious' scene in *Notting Hill* where Hugh Grant was in the cinema wearing a diving mask, that's where it was filmed. Initially they had people smoking in it, but they had to be removed, because Americans apparently couldn't cope with the fact that you could still smoke in a cinema. Typical...

robram

My local pub has recently started doing film nights where you can not only smoke but also drink and enjoy bowls of olives and home-made hummus and all for a fiver! The films shown are fairly unusual (last weekend was a Buster Keaton short and then *Calamity Jane* and next time it's *Arsenic and Old Lace*) but the organisers are always asking for suggestions for upcoming weeks and seem genuinely open to ideas.

It's also a great chance to meet some genuine (i.e. eccentric) Londoners – last week's cowboy fashion show was a sight to behold...

Full details can be found at www.fabfilmco.org.uk where they also have details of other events for those of you too scared to make the hike down to the depths of south London (Gipsy Hill).

🗩 **K8LN**

Victoriana

My husband and I just had the most incredible weekend at Miller's residence in Notting Hill and I cannot recommend it highly enough. It's not youth-hostel-cheap but neither is it sell-your-kidney-expensive. Note if you like modern minimalist chic then this is not the place for you. It is crammed, and I mean crammed, with antiques, memorabilia, Victoriana – you see something new every time you go into the salon/lounge or walk through the place and in your room. I have never encountered such a chilled, comfortable, charming and friendly hotel.

It was my 30th birthday and we requested a bottle of champagne which we received at no charge. There are bowls with mountains of candy and chocolate throughout the hotel and in your room, and there is a free bar. Yes, that says 'free', for all the guests to use. We opted to stay in the hotel when we weren't out at dinner just to enjoy the surroundings in the guest lounge. Breakfast starts at 8am and was still out at

midday (when we got up and went downstairs) and not an eyebrow was raised. The 'Byron Room' has a four-poster bed :-) Check it out at www.millersuk.com (and book through Lastminute.com where they have deals!).

💬 Jodie

Fire

Is there a conspiracy against Bonfire Night in north London? When I first moved here aeons ago we had two massive firework displays to choose from in Highbury Fields and Primrose Hill. First they moved the Highbury one to Finsbury Park and then merged it with the one in Ally Pally and then they cancelled the Primrose Hill one. South London's awash with displays from Clapham and Streatham commons, but we have Ally Pally or nothing. Bah!

💬 Highbury gal

It is probably because fireworks displays consume vast amounts of public cash and because Ally Pally is the best place in the whole of London to watch fireworks because you can also watch everyone else's!

Little known Ally Pally facts:

1. It has an old POW camp from WW11 under it.
2. It is the main communications centre for spying on Londoners. (The police are up the big tower, and have a camera that can read your door number from about 5 miles away.)
3. It is completely overrun by wild cats.

4. The huge dilapidated back rooms include one of the
    first stages used by the BBC which still has all the old
    mixing kit in there, massive rotting red curtains etc.
    and it is all rather majestic and sad.

I absolutely love Ally Pally! It is probably still crap inside
because the council keeps throwing all the money up
in the air!

🗨 thetotateeteetotaofeeyore

That's a neat trick if your door faces south, say. And what
do you mean? I imagine some sort of little police station
hundreds of metres in the air, with bobbies in hats wandering
around, drinking cups of tea, looking out of the windows
with binoculars and muttering 'Now then, now then'…

🗨 Tiddles

Rhythm by London

King

Just driven down the Old Kent Road and spotted
a restaurant called *Elvis Gracelands Palace Chinese
Restaurant*. Looked interesting but wanted to ask
if anybody had been there and did they have a
real Elvis? If not anybody know where I can get some
food and some live Elvis (will travel, big fan)?

🗨 Dorflbob

The *Graceland* restaurant on Old Kent Road was the venue
for one of my all-time top ten evenings out in London. If you
do a group booking (i.e. spend a bit) the aged restaurant

owner will leap into his jumpsuit and regale you with an Elvis Tribute show. He seems to completely ignore the fact that he's an elderly Chinese man with faltering English and no musical talent and so will you because his dedication is actually quite moving; it's all deadly serious, his personal tribute to the King thank you very much. It is a few years ago so I do hope the old trooper is still going strong and hasn't heaven forbid sold out to some restaurant chain. But ring and ask. Tell them Mike asked after them.

💬 Mike

Elvis Gracelands Palace Chinese Restaurant is one of four owned by Paul 'Elvis' Chan, who comes out (or sometimes other Chinese Elvis impersonators – Paul can't be everywhere every night!) hips a-shaking and arms a-swinging dressed in white lycra and flared trousers *à la* 'late period Elvis', singing all those classic Elvis numbers with a Chinese accent while you munch on your Cantonese cuisine. I went to his Tunbridge Wells restaurant, and it was one of the more surreal meals in my life! Highly recommended as oddball entertainment. They can't really sing, the food is average but totally edible and tasty Chinese, and they're so enthusiastic you can't help but enjoy it!

💬 Elvis' Burger

Cheese

I'm looking for a cheesy night out of dancing in central/north London location. We want to have a good time, we are not out to see or be seen, pay for overpriced cocktails, or listen to obscure music from DJs who love themselves. Nor do we want to stick to the floor in *Walkabout*, thank you.

I have Googled it and best bet so far seems to be 'Silver Bob's Disco Meltdown' at the *Old Red Lion*, which broadly seems to fit the bill. Any opinions on this or other suggestions very gratefully received.

⌐ **Cheesemeister**

The Cheesemeister should try 'Guilty Pleasures', a monthly club night at the *Islington Carling Academy*. Like the name suggests it's a night where all and sundry are encouraged to bring along the rogue Foreigner albums etc. lingering in their record collections and dance like a mad thing (handbags on the floor are optional).

⌐ **Highbury Gal**

'Shake' at the *Camden Electric Ballroom* is as Gorgonzola as it gets: www.electric-ballroom.co.uk/shake.htm.

⌐ **Griff**

In response to Cheesemeister's search, the *Carling Academy* is good for a bit of cheese and really quite cheap too. The Xfm night (first Friday of the month I think) is really good, quite rock and indie but it does get quite packed even though it's a pretty huge club. If you're looking for something a little more intimate then *Buffalo* bar (just under *The Famous Cock*, next to Highbury station) has a good vibe and again is reasonably priced. Good luck with your night out!

⌐ **Z**

Maturing

My friends and I have a problem. We've all been in the big city for a while, and we've had a fantastic time, but most of our weekends revolve around going out clubbing, getting caned and not sleeping much. We're all feeling the pace, and recently when we were having yet another early morning conversation, the following question floated to the top of the barrel...

What could we do, at weekends, in or near London that is (a) cheap, as we're skint, (b) interesting and varied and likely to appeal to most if not all of us, (c) healthy, (d) outdoorsy, (e) not too strenuous in the initial stages as we're all not what you'd call fit, and (f) enough of a laugh that we'd want to do it again and wouldn't instantly be drawn back to the lasers, pills and lager? We've thought of all the usual suspects, hillwalking, surfing, canoeing, paintball etc. Anyone got a really random hobby they want to share with us?

TiredAndEmotional

I know exactly how you feel. Thankfully I'm not tired of the weekend scene yet, but have been putting in the groundwork for when I inevitably will do...

Off the back of an earlier LbL post, I signed up with the chaps at www.cityskate.co.uk for a beginner's course in rollerblading. They were wonderful, and £100 and five weeks later I'm able to go quite fast on the city streets without falling over. Their Friday night skates look a bit too advanced for me, but they do a rollerstroll every Sunday, promising a relaxed skate around London, with different routes each week. Once you're trained and have your own stuff, it's completely free, a great way to meet new 20-/30-somethings, and it's good for you without you needing to be fit in the first place. Either that, or you could just go for a pint and a fry-up which is what I will be doing until the weather turns rollerblading-friendly.

🗩 **Gizzard**

Tap

 Does anyone know of somewhere in Central London/SE that does tap dance classes for beginners? Have seen a number of musicals recently which have revived my childhood dreams of tapping!

🗩 **hannahbanana**

Check out *Morley College* in Lambeth. My friend and I have just done a year's beginner's tap course. Really good fun and you get to do a couple of shows a year. Monday nights at six.

🗩 **Cazza**

Pineapple (Langley Street, Covent Garden) has the best beginner's class I know. Look for a teacher called Junior, he breaks it all down in a fun and easy way. Also, if you are 26 or under, go to www.wac.co.uk. They're based in Belsize Park.

🗩 **sparkleshark**

Danceworks in Balderton Street (opposite *Selfridges* department store clock) offers one or two beginner's ballet classes every day. In the classes I have been to, students are of all ages, literally from 12 to 70, and the classes are well-corrected. Each class costs £5 plus a £4 day-member's charge. So £9 in total. HOWEVER if you become a member, (£59 joining fee plus £6.99 a month, you pay just £5 per class) AND THE GOOD NEWS IS, if you join in September, there's no £59 joining fee to pay! So go ahead, get yo tutu on and pile on down there.

🗩 **speeler**

Blues

 Just heard of a bar somewhere in the West End called 'Ain't Nothing But the Blues'. Apparently, as the name would suggest, it's a bar where the blues is played every night. Anyone know if this is true have you been there at all; is it any good; what types of blues; when are the best nights?

🗩 **Syzygy**

You're thinking of *Ain't Nothin But*, the blues bar on Kingly Street in behind *Liberty* in the West End. You can visit their website at www.aintnothinbut.co.uk. It's tiny so be prepared to get squashed if it's busy, or get there early to get one of the few tables. The music has been good the couple of times I've been there but I'm no blues specialist. Also try dinner first at the fantastic *Shampers* at the other end of Kingly Street excellent food and a great wine list (I'd recommend the Dogajolo red), though usually packed so make sure you book.

🗩 **Lizardbath**

Ain't Nothing But does indeed play nothing but the blues.
The performances I've seen there have been quite good.
However, the experience has been tempered by some
of the rudest bar staff I've ever encountered. I've since
decided to never go back. There are other places to hear
the blues in London...

💬 Chz

Busk

The Carling-sponsored busking seems to have
nosedived. There is an *appalling* Chinese girl wailing
and strumming a guitar every evening at London
Bridge station as you change onto the Jubilee line.
Actually she sounds more like she is grumbling/moaning and
she's the last thing you want to hear on your way home.

💬 sellers

I too pass through London Bridge on a daily basis and have
been shocked by the 'appalling' Chinese busker who is
indeed atrocious. But believe it or not, worse is in store.
Last night, in the Chinese girl's spot, there was a male/
female duet doing what I can only describe as a sort of
cross between folk and opera. Lots of yelling and trilling.
Actually, I can't describe it. I can't do justice to how
horrendous it was. It was almost like an operatic madrigal.
You also ought to know that the female half of the duo was
wearing red and black trousers with vertical stripes, and
when the male half saw me standing, staring dumbstruck
with horror he winked at me. Urgh.

💬 bad girl bubby

DJ

I'm getting married in London next year, and don't know where to start looking for a DJ. We're worried that we're going to end up with a dodgy bloke mumbling away over his old record collection. We just need to find someone nice and experienced who would take a bit of time to find out what we want, so that we can relax and get on with the dancing.

Gilly

My superstar DJ friend Ben is who you're looking for. As nice and as talented as they come, he plays 60s/70s funk and soul with some of the more upbeat disco tunes thrown in for good groove measure. He also has a penchant for early bebop/hiphop. He plays at several clubs and bars in Bristol, but mainly packs the dancefloor at weddings and mates' parties. The man can do no wrong. I spent last weekend shakin my ass to his choons til the sun came up. You can reach him at the world's fiddliest email address: Ben.Liddiard@avon-somerset.probation.gsx.gov.uk. Happy wedding disco.

Dumb Brunette

I can do that very adequately indeed, and frequently do. I'll give you music that's familiar without ever being cheesy; you'll give me money, we'll both be happy. I can supply references to back up all claims. Get in touch: dirtysuedj@yahoo.co.uk.

Dirty Sue

I know a DJ who is pretty cool. Will play pretty much whatever you want, although has an extensive range of stuff,
so I am sure you could come to some agreement. DJ Pioneer
contact jon.scott@cyrilsweett.com

⌐⌐ **The Secret Person**

In Soho, next door to *Ronnie Scott's* is the *Soho Arts Club*.
It's run and DJ-ed by Rulie who used to play in Whitesnake
and is quite a character. We booked him as our wedding
DJ and he plays anything you want but really can keep the
party going and is a lovely guy. Try him.

⌐⌐ **Gavin**

Literature by London

Poetry

I have Googled this, but without some sort of
recommendation, it's a bit arduous to try and go to
the 20 or so venues in and around London to find the
best one. So, I put it to my learned friends: Where is
the best café/bar for one to go and see live poetry readings?

A few words of context. I've never done this before,
and have never had the slightest interest in poetry. But I've
made some 'discoveries' lately (read 'Wilde') and I'd like
to try it on, so to speak. I don't want to DO any reading,
just sit, listen, and sip an Earl Grey or a beer, and maybe
chit-chat to fellow poetry people between stanzas.
Any recommendations? Central to 'Near West' (Not Heathrow!)
is best for me, but have Oyster, will travel for quality!

⌐⌐ **mudge**

The *Poetry Cafe* in Betterton Street (www.poetrysociety.org.uk/
cafe/cafeind.htm) would probably suit. I met a friend there
recently for a glass of wine and watched as friendly-looking
people arrived to read and be read to. The street isn't very
promising, but the cafe is really nice.

💬 **Anna**

The *Poetry Library*, at the South Bank Centre, is good for poetry
readings and finding more poetry: www.poetrylibrary.org.uk.

💬 **Mr Chat**

Hey mudge, if it's live poetry you're after, look no further than
'Book Slam' at *Cherry Jam* (W2) on the last Thursday of every
month. As the blurb says, 'It's a monthly spoken word and music
night with host, author and hip hop journalist, Patrick Neate
(Whitbread Prize Winner 2001). Expect readings, mellow funk and
social vibes. Previous guests at this superb night have included
Monica Ali, Nick Hornby, Tariq Goddard, Paul Morley, Malika
Booker, Kim Trusty, DJ Touche, Mahogony Brown, Jive Poetic,
Jake Arnott, Netsayi, David Henry Sterry and more.' Well, quite.
  The next one's on 31st March – in the words of Leslie
Crowther, come on down...

💬 **ils**

Books

Who knows of some decent bookshops in town,
proper bookshops, not your common garden
Waterstones? Ones full of books that smell as old
as they look! Not necessarily looking for originals
or valuable books but ones with more character than the
mass-produced Penguin Classics?

💬 **Kenningtom**

Here are some good bookshops. None of them are near Kennington, I'm afraid, but why not make a day of it with my handy travel guide?

Skoob books (Tavistock Square, www.skoob.com) and *Judd Books* (182 Marchmont Street). Conveniently located opposite *Judd Books* is the *Lord John Russell* pub. It's a fine pub but don't slag off Leeds FC because Dave the Landlord will tear off your limbs with his teeth.

Halcyon Books, 1 Greenwich South Street, directly opposite tube station. Arguably the best place for second-hand fiction in London. Afterwards why not climb the hill, look at the magnificent view and have a can or two of Super.

Couple on Stoke Newington Church Street. Other activities could include wandering mournful Abney Cemetery or playing backgammon in the *Fox Reformed*.

Foyles and others on Charing Cross Road. The heart of London's famous bookland, *Foyles* was once infamous for its unhelpful staff. The staff are still unhelpful but *Foyles* is no longer infamous.

Book stalls by *NFT*. Overpriced and always a slightly disappointing selection, but can't be faulted for convenience.

Housmans, 5 Caledonian Road. A solid gold institution: sued for libel in 2002 by anti-gay litigant for stocking a pamphlet accusing him of plagiarism he was eventually awarded just £14. Sells general remainders and radical-left stuff, with a huge basement full of yellowing treatises on the dialectical materialism from the point of view of Welsh lamb farmers etc. For afters, pop over to the delightful *Flying Scotsman* for a bit of radical rough and tumble fun.

Books for Amnesty International, 139b King Street, Hammersmith. So far as anyone can tell, there are no other good reasons to go to Hammersmith but if you do find yourself there, I think there's a *Tesco Metro* by the tube station.

◻ Ippy

Wall

Hi, I am lucky enough to have acquired a decently sized room at uni next year, but am eager to decorate the walls with some nice prints/posters. All sorts of things spring to mind though vintage film prints, and specifically Fahrenheit 451 or anything by Francois Truffaut, but the main thing is I want something really big, sort of bus-stop poster size, and most internet sites only offer smaller posters. Does anyone know of any good sites or art shops that might help?

◻ Jonesey

If you really want the coolest wall in studentdom, cash your loan cheque and spend a wad on www.polishposter.com. The Poles hire artists to make their posters and they're all great. The American film posters are a bit pricey but the theatre ones are wicked. Or, if you want something cheaper and yet equally impressive, choose your favourite image and rasturbate it at http://homokaasu.org/rasterbator. Then all you need is the uni laser printer and some blu-tack. Plenty of ideas in their gallery, too.

◻ C-Bob

Bookshare

One of my friends mentioned to me the other week that there was a website where you could look up where people have left any books they've just read apparently they tell you where they've left read books in London and if they're still there you can pick them up, read them and then leave them wherever you finish them, then posting the location on the website. This sounded like quite a nice idea to me, but unfortunately she doesn't remember the website and I can't find it on Google – has anyone heard of it?

Juicy

The website is *BookCrossing* (www.bookcrossing.com) and it is indeed a nice idea. Basically, when you have read a book rather than putting it back on the shelf to collect dust the site encourages you to review it and register it, write in a unique ID number and then leave it somewhere bus, cafe, park bench, toilet, museum, anywhere really. Then when someone picks up the book they can go to the website, type in the number and find out who had that book before them and what they thought of it. There are lots of active BookCrossers in London and there are regular meets where members meet up to exchange books and have a natter and a drink. It's as much a social hobby as a literary one and great fun.

chelseagirl

I feel like a complete miseryguts for writing this especially when BookCrossing sounds so cool and something I would normally go for 200% but I think it has to be said that leaving things about on the tube, buses etc. ain't a good thing. This morning there was a poster in my tube station that said that in the last week alone (i.e. post the terrorist attacks) 100 items had been left unattended on the tube. On my journey home last night the carriage was littered with empty cans and rubbish. I'm not normally a paranoid type but for a second I couldn't help glancing at the stuff lying around. And of course we get delays if a suspect package is reported. I know: books look like books so shouldn't be a problem, I just think we should be (over) abiding by the rules at the mo. Agh I hate this!

🗩 Caroline393

I was a little concerned about leaving books lying around too but you don't have to leave them on the tube and I've put the sticker on the front of the book so if you do see it and freak out you can read the label and realise it's meant to be left lying around. You can always leave it in a coffee shop or supermarket or just on the wall outside your house.

🗩 whatever

Leisure by London

Horse

In my (not so long ago) youth I used to be a reasonably accomplished horse rider. I have recently been considering taking the up the reins again and whilst I would love to be able to afford to buy and stable a horse in London, it just isn't going to happen. Does anyone know of any good riding schools in north London where I can get some good tuition/hacks, on nice horses that doesn't cost the earth?

🗩 Jenn

The *Trent Park Riding Stables* near Oakwood tube station is very good. The lessons are about £25 an hour but it's one to one/one to two tuition and they are very accomplished tutors who will take you on hacks through nearby Trent Park which is a very nice big space for the odd gallop.

💬 **Horsey Horserson**

There's a great stables in between Leyton and Clapton called Lee Valley Riding Stables on the Lee Bridge Road. They're really friendly and have an open door so you can just show up and take a look around, meet the horses and staff etc. whenever you like. The Lee Valley is a lovely area with canals and nature reserves aplenty – we loved it!

💬 **cozmokaty**

Volley

 Is there anywhere to play beach volleyball in London?

💬 **Spike**

The pub next to our house has a volleyball court in the beer garden and when the weather perks up there's always lots of activity. A good way to combine pints and fun stuff! It's the *Royal Albert* on St Stephen's Terrace, Vauxhall and worth a look in by non-volleyballers too!

💬 **Mary**

You can play beach volleyball at *Zulu's* in Leytonstone. It's a pub, but the beer garden has been covered with sand and there is a volleyball net there. I think it's only open in summer, but there are always people playing when it's hot.

🗨 **Leytonstone Boy**

I'm informed by my volleyball-fanatic friend that there's an indoor centre at Upper Heyford (Oxfordshire way), and an outdoor court at the *Acton Lido*.

Otherwise check out www.beachvolleyball.org.uk for all the summer UK events.

🗨 **JooPoo**

Dunk

Does anyone know of a friendly basketball club in south-west London? I haven't played for a few years but would love to get back into it. Not looking for anything too serious, just the chance to train and enjoy the sport again.

🗨 **Neverbeenabletodunk**

There is a turn up and play session (£5 for two hours) in Victoria on Wednesday evenings at the *Queen Mother's Sports Centre*, 8.10pm. The standard of players varies from really bad to pretty good, teams change each week and except for one or two people with attitude issues all of those that go are chilled-out, friendly people who simply like playing ball.

🗨 **ginger ninja**

Golf

I've been browsing the net recently for 'different' things to do in town without much luck. I came across *Urban Golf* (www.urbangolf.co.uk) which I thought looked cool... Can anyone shed some light?

🗩 **spandangle**

I went to the Urban Golf place for a friend's birthday earlier this year... it is indeed a strange place and really hard to find. It's not signposted and is literally a buzzer on a normal looking door in a lane off of Old Compton Street. We had to ring the place for directions after walking around lost for half an hour!

Inside it is pretty funky, but definitely aimed at people who can actually play golf. You hire out a booth, which has a whole course projected onto a screen it seems to be Microsoft-driven software and is pretty impressive. You have a full set of clubs and a various 'mats' which are supposed to be relevant to different surfaces sand, grass etc. They serve beer and wine to your table and the staff were really nice to us... especially considering none of us could play golf and one of us made a pretty good attempt at breaking through to the next cubicle with a 9-iron. Two hours cost us about 30 quid each, and although we were all shite, it was a good laugh.

🗩 **Clefty**

Crazy golf is a wonderful pastime (no honestly, it is!). It reminds me of holidays and while playing in the Spanish sunshine might be a great deal more appealing than playing in London smog, I think it qualifies as a 'different' thing to do. There's a nine-hole crazy golf course at Alexandra Palace and an 'adventure' golf course in Broomfield Park, N13. Adventure golf!! Now that sounds different! I haven't been to any of these courses; I meant to plan a trip for my birthday but forgot (going to the dogs instead) so when a sunny day arrives I think I'll be off. I'll let you all know what it's like.

Info can be found at www.miniaturegolfer.com/eng_courses.html.

🗨 **Big Sis**

Yoga

Can anyone recommend any 'holiday time' yoga courses in the city that aren't too expensive (around the £5 mark)?

🗨 **anon**

Check out *Yoga Junction* right next to Finsbury Park station. Most classes are more like £9 but there are a few cheaper options:

- 'Community classes' at £4 each.
- Free classes run by trainee teachers (who are on the BWY diploma course so even while they are trainees probably have a vastly greater knowledge of yoga than your average instructor down the gym!).

Their website at www.yogajunction.co.uk has details, timetable and so on. They do various different styles, and every teacher I've had there has been lovely, knowledgeable, friendly and basically everything you could hope for in a yoga teacher.

🗨 **WorldGirl**

The *Bhavan Centre* (*Insitute of Indian Art and Culture*)
in West Kensington have yoga lessons on Monday to
Thursday after work. I find the Tuesday level suits me best,
just about strenuous enough without causing me distress.
Each hour-long session costs £5. Their website is
www.bhavan.net. Have a go!

💬 **barmaid**

Bike

**I want to buy a second-hand bike which hasn't
just been stolen. Any suggestion for reputable
seond-hand bicycle dealers (preferably central,
or west London)?**

💬 **andrew**

Psubliminal, 17 Balham High Road, Balham, SW12 9AJ.
Sorry, it's not particularly local but it is very good. I went
there after I had my bike stolen and they were fantastic,
took details of my bike just in case anyone tried to sell it
on to them, gave me a test ride, cut down the seat post
so it was the right height. Everytime I go in (even if its
just for new batteries for my lights) they do something
for me like pump the tyres up or sort out a squeak. I never
ask them to, they just confiscate my bike on the way in
and don't give it back until it's perfect and they never charge
for these additional tweaks.

💬 **Honeybaby**

Try *Gee Whiz* in Fulham Broadway – fairly small workshop
but there are enough bikes packed in there to provide
some choice. I've bought two bikes from there (thanks to

the thieving bastard that stole the first one) and have been very happy with both.

💬 **Christoff van Rensburger**

I've said it before on LbL, but am happy to once again recommend *Re:Cycling* of the Elephant & Castle. It's in the arches under the railway line behind the shopping centre: fairly central and you can ride home again (if all goes well). As the name implies, they deal in second-hand bikes. They've been doing it for at least half a dozen years, so you know they're legit. Most of the bikes come from police auctions, apparently. Nice guys offering unpatronising service and decent deals on guaranteed bikes.

💬 **ninorc**

I suggest checking out your local council actually. I live in Walthamstow and Waltham Forest council recycling dept actually has an official 'bike recycle' scheme. They are situated next to the tip (handily) and if you live in the borough you can buy a bike every first Saturday of the month. Depending on the size, expect to pay around £35 for a perfect working bike which has been recycled for you by volunteers.

In addition, they employ a bike mechanic two days a week who will teach you how to look after your own bike (gears, brake cables, tyres etc.) for nowt pence AND riding instructors who run free group classes or private instruction on road riding and safety. Which is also free!!

Yet another reason to live in Walthamstow...

💬 **phatflaresback**

And finally

Mushrooms

It's been a dreadfully long time and I have decided that I desperately need to squeegee my third eye, and if I'm not mistaken (I may well be) we are in the midst of the mushroom picking season, so now is the time. What I'd like to know is if there are any decent places in London to pick psilocybin mushrooms.

There must be. I'm really hoping a trip to Dartmoor won't be necessary, because if it is, it won't happen. And there's nothing illegal about this, as there will be no 'alteration by the hand of man', so just in case any of you were about to, please don't get your knickers in a twist.

💬 **Callan**

I've heard that Richmond Park can be a good spot for finding the odd mushroom, apparently...

💬 **Willy**

On Sunday I joined a foraging trip for mushrooms and toadstools, at four sites around Haringey. This was superb fun, and has made me feel twenty times better about paying council tax (it was free and organised by the council).

Turns out the conditions are perfect this year, and we found dozens of different species, e.g. blewitts, false death caps, the weird Jews ears. All ably identified and explained by the expert mycologists who also rule on what's edible. Best of all, my girlfriend found the ultra-rare, £60 per kilo

boletus in Ally Pally. Before you ask, she 'can't remember' which tree they were growing under... The only psychedelic mushrooms we found were also rather poisonous, unless filtered via reindeer-urine first. The day ended with a fry-up of the spoils with garlic on French bread. Top class.
Other forays are at: www.wildlondon.org.uk/events.php.

And before anyone complains apparently the fungi actually like having their tops picked off. They're mostly underground, you know.

⌐ **ATP**

Callan – bit late for picking mushies now, but Epping Forest is a top spot. Better yet, since the Old Bill has given the green light to the selling of fresh mushrooms, there are lots of places to get them. Head along Camden High Street towards the market (you can't miss the vendors) and price compare. Pick somewhere that will give you advice on type and dosage; I recommend the golden cap/golden top varieties.

⌐ **Terence**

Transport

Leonard Cohen once sang, 'There is a crack in everything; that's how the light gets in.' We feel absolutely certain that what he meant by this was, 'Sure, London Transport is frequently unreliable and dirty; the staff can be  breathtakingly stupid and rude; and the price of a one-day travelcard is enough to make you spit – but let's face it, if it wasn't so downright grotty and repulsive, we probably wouldn't have the enormous pleasure of bus conductors that play harmonica or speak in rhyming couplets; punters that share cabs home and... erm, the tube mice.' In this section Londoners dissect London's transport system; the good and the bad, the disgusting and the inefficient.

London by Underground

Heart-warming

I saw a heart-warming thing on the tube the other day that I thought I would share with you all. It was in the middle of a particularly stuffy afternoon on a stalled Northern line train outside of King's Cross. The carriage was about half-full and a woman in her 50s started to cough. At first it seemed like quite a ticklish cough, but it kept going and increasing in volume until it was a big scary barking thing. There was a man in a suit sitting next to her who I could see wanted desperately to move away but probably felt too embarrassed. He was covering his mouth with his hand but trying to do it slyly. Then at exactly the same time, two people from different places in the carriage produced bottles of water which they then offered the coughing woman. One of them had a small unopened bottle which she gave the woman. The woman was very grateful. Then the man in the suit surprised me by offering the woman a Polo mint. Then the train moved into the station and I got off feeling a bit ashamed, as I was just about the only one who hadn't tried to help. But apart from my shame, it was a lovely moment.

💬 Bella

Since when did giving a choking woman a sip of water and a Polo count as heart-warming? Common courtesy surely. I suggest the poster remembers that commuting isn't the real world and reminds himself/herself how people treat each other when they interact normally...

💬 mikecarterinlondon

I think that's the point. Ordinary people turn into complete twunts when commuting (me included on occasion, I'm ashamed to say) and it is heart-warming to be reminded that people can do nice things for no reason sometimes. I, for one, felt a little warm glow.

💬 Kaymonster

Reply

As a tube driver, I would like to say how touching it is to hear from the people who seem to be somewhat fair in their judgements of London Underground. There are a lot of things I would like to put across but as usual you can't convince everybody. Firstly, how many of you get randomly tested for drugs and alcohol at your work place? How many of you wake up at 3am on a Sunday to go to work? You can slag us off all you like but come Monday morning you all rush to stuff yourselves into the trains (all 3 million of you) like tinned sardines and trust us with your lives. Well I hope you can rest assured that the drivers and station staff are not hungover or stoned out of their heads (like some of the pilots who fly or attempt to do so.) Mind the crap.

💬 tube driver

Jubilee noise

Does anyone know why Jubilee line trains make that weird noise as they pull out of stations? Its similar to the noise any accelerating electric train would make, except it's repetitive, like someone playing a sample of the sound on a loop. It can't be because of the extra set of doors, as it also happens on stations that don't have them.

faking girl

The noise made by the Jubilee line rolling stock is simply the gear-changing noise as the train accelerates or slows down as it departs/enters a platform. On a similar note, has anyone else noticed that the chime played by Jubilee trains as the doors open at a station sounds like the beginning of the *Sesame Street* theme tune?

enfant terrible

Tube trains are electric – they don't have gears, so it's not the gears changing. What it is is to do with the use of gate turn-off (GTO) thyristors in the traction control system. I have no idea what such a thing is, nor why it should make a noise like that, but I want to believe it anyway. Apparently, Northern line trains, which are otherwise very similar, use more modern insulated gate bipolar transistor (IGBT) power electronics, which don't make the noise. So now you know.

tom

Your post reminded me to ask the LbL readership if anyone has heard another noise made by Jubilee line trains. I can

only describe the noise as the sound of running water.
It's as if you're the other side of a very thin wall and
someone's just flushed the loo in the next room. The noise
seems to travel from one end of the carriage to the other
and yet no one on the carriage bats an eyelid at this
seemingly (super-) natural sound. Has anyone else heard
it and do they know what it is?

🗨 dominic

The noise you describe is indeed running water, the '96
stock, like all the modern stock on the Underground,
is fabricated from an extruded aluminium body with a plastic
inner shell that forms the interior of the carriage. There is
a space between this shell and the actual body of the train
to accommodate the air ventilation and wiring for the lights
and other systems. On some carriages the roof has not been
sealed properly and rain water has seeped into this space;
this is what you hear moving about when the train is
moving and braking.

🗨 Chris

I've also noticed the familiar chiming noise when the
doors open on the Jubilee line, and many a time I've found
myself humming the *Sesame Street* theme song all the way
home! Also, has anyone else noticed that the handrail on
all Jubilee line escalators move faster than the actual
moving steps? I've never noticed it on any other line,
but I find it really annoying!

🗨 east acton gal

To reply to east acton gal, the handle on most escalators
that I've experienced moves faster than the steps for a

reason that I'm not entirely sure of, but an educated guess would be that the wheel that the handle is wrapped around is larger than the wheel that operates the steps, and due to this size difference it affects the revolution speed, so the larger handle wheel has to rotate slower than the step wheel to compensate for the rpm difference, and I suppose the timing is just out kinda like the two cogs on a bike; you peddle the same but the smaller cog at the back spins like a nutter while the larger cog at the front gently ambles around. But who really cares eh? And I suppose in a week or two some other smartass will correct me. Take the stairs, stairs are good. No complicated machinery or potential life-or-death situations at the top and a free workout.

🗨 **Londoner on tour Down Under**

In response to east acton gal, the handrails on all of the escalators have to move faster than the steps. They have further to travel to do a complete loop than the stairs themselves.

🗨 **Penfold**

Service

I recently emailed LUL to ask them about their policy regarding the wording on the whiteboards they use in most tube stations to inform passengers of the status of services on all lines. I queried the widespread and irksome use of 'good service' to denote an absence of delays. Whether it's a good service or not is a subjective matter and surely only the paying passengers should be the judge of it. Is a good service on the Jubilee

line (mean waiting time: 5 mins) really the same as a
good service on the Victoria line (2 mins), for example?
Surely, I suggested, it should be 'normal' or 'OK'.
The response I received was that 'good service' is easier
for foreign passengers to understand. But 'no delays' means
that they have to understand only two words to get the
full picture, I argued. Answer came there none.

🖵 Llamapiss

The phrase 'normal service' was phased out on the London
Underground signage by none other than Mayor Ken
Livingstone. The idea was that 'good service' sounded
better, was easier for tourists to read and makes people
more confident about their journeys. Also the fact that the
phrase 'normal service' led many to expect delays.

🖵 enfant terrible

On the subject of inappropriate messages at tube stations,
I was amused and annoyed in equal parts when the platform
indicator at Canary Wharf told me that the East London line
had 'a good service with delays'.

🖵 JooPoo

Exciting

**I heard an announcement in Euston Underground
station this morning: 'code 3 on platform 6,
code 3 on platform 6'. How exciting! A code 3!
What's a code 3?**

🖵 Creep is Rubbish

I believe a code 3 call means that someone has thrown up on the platform. It is probably somewhat more pleasant an announcement than 'Bucket and mop to platform 6 please'.

☐ Pete

Turnham green (with envy)

Does anyone else get annoyed that Piccadilly trains don't stop at Turnham Green except at useless times? I don't know why they don't and I drive the damn things. I'd be interested to know how many people would like us to stop there.

☐ Dream Monkey

I certainly would! Especially when the District line is being rubbish – it's so frustrating when everybody's crowded on the platform and nearly-empty Piccadilly line trains trundle past. Sometimes trains do stop when there are delays on the District line, but this seems to be very rare. But if they can stop at Turnham Green why not at Ravenscourt Park it's got the platforms for it, were they ever used? Stamford Brook's got a westbound Piccadilly-facing platform too, but not an eastbound one.

☐ Alex

I don't know about Turnham Green but I would *love* the Piccadilly line to stop at Ravenscourt Park station (two stops east). I sometimes have to see five Piccadilly trains go by before a District line train picks me up.

☐ Raven

A few months ago I was at Ravenscourt Park station and a Piccadilly line train came in on the District line tracks and picked up passengers! It then continued along the normal Piccadilly route afterwards. Has anyone else had similar experiences?

⌐ **Goldhawk Gal**

Chiswick residents have been campaigning for years to get Piccadilly line trains to stop at Turnham Green station during the day. I think Transport for London, backed by the Mayor, is opposed to the plan because it will reduce the overall service on the line. As a TG resident, I know how frustrating it is to watch three or four trains speed past before the District line trundles up, but I can see their point. Every stop adds a couple of minutes to the service, which over the course of a day would add up to less trains. Presumably they make the same argument for Stamford Brook and Ravenscourt Park. And let's face it: these stations are all within spitting distance of each other and are served by an adequate (albeit slower) service already. I think there are more important things to worry about on the tube, like why the Northern line can't run for a single day without signal failures.

⌐ **fluffy mark**

Whistle

On the tube every morning, as I leave Earl's Court on the District line, Barons Court-bound, I see the rather quaint sight of a trackside sign, saying 'Whistle!'. Surely there aren't any trains that can whistle any more. Is this for the benefit of the track maintenance staff? Are there secret steam trains still running on the lines at night doing an Ivor the Engine? Can anyone explain?

💬 robram

I can assure you that all the tube trains are fitted with whistles. The Central line trains in particular always whistle when exiting the tunnel eastbound just before Leyton station, not sure why that is mind you. It can be a good way to entertain young children to take them to a railway bridge and wave at the train driver who nine times out of ten will whistle back!

💬 enfant terrible

The whistle boards that you see around the Underground network are in fact in use and they remind us drivers to blow the whistle to alert anyone who may be on the track (a lot of maintenance people love to go walkabout, especially on nice sunny days). And it may surprise you to learn that we have whistles on every train powered by compressed air which is also used for a lot of other things like operating the doors. On the line that I drive on we have particularly loud whistles.

💬 tubeguru

Smile

Last night on my way home on the District line, from Earl's Court to Wimbledon, it was the usual throng of people on the cattle train. Anyhoo, I usually play this simple game – I smile at people and see what reaction I get. 99% of the time, I am stared at as though I have two heads or I am some alien lifeform from Mars, their mouths don't even twitch. However, last night, there was this blonde girl sitting with her boyfriend, and our eyes met and I received such a warm glowing smile from her, it was truly fantastic and made me feel so happy, that I smiled even more than I usually do.

So basically my point is, PLEASE SMILE people, I know life out there is hard, but believe me, if you have a smile on your face, it affects other people, lights them up and keeps them going, and if Blonde girl reads this, I just want to say Thank YOU!

💬 Giovanni

Arrogant

Getting onto a very crowded tube at London Bridge this morning, I was forced against a very rude and arrogant suit who was standing rigid to give himself more space. When asked to move he told me I should waited for another tube! What's the best way to deal with such selfish people?

💬 tubeangry

Perhaps you should take a deep breath, pause, and consider whether you weren't the selfish one. You say that the 'suit' (the fact that you used this expression suggests a certain contempt for them) was 'standing rigid'. Did you expect this person to crumple into a ball in the corner in order to make you more comfortable? Perhaps you should direct your anger at the Government who seem unable or unwilling to provide adequate public transport capacity. Of course, it's a lot easier to just turn on each other isn't it?

💬 The Mediator

Instead of getting on the tube at London Bridge (which is an effing nightmare and has been for the last three years) why not get off and get the bus instead? I can heartily recommend the number 17 which goes all the way to Kings Cross and is a far more agreeable mode of transport. Top deck, able to watch those city types scurrying to work. Heaven, and no contorting your body or briefcases jammed up your arse... unless you prefer that kind of thing.

💬 Sellers

Dark

Travelling home up the Victoria line on Monday, the carriage lights throughout the train went out at Tottenham Hale station. With only five of us in the carriage, by the dimming light of the station as we departed, one of the guys gave a bemused smile. The train turned pitch black as we disappeared into the tunnel, and two other guys started running around screaming – for a laugh, it seems. It occurred

to me that I didn't know exactly where to find the red alarm handle, and that I didn't want to pull it as we'd all want to get home anyway, without stopping a dark train in a tunnel.

Come Blackhorse Road, numerous passengers left the train as though nothing was unusual. Spurred on by wine and adrenalin, not to mention the danger of travelling from Tottenham to Walthamstow in complete darkness, I ran up the platform shouting 'Oi, driver!', at which point a woman appeared at the cab window, blissfully unaware as she pulled out the earplugs. The driver was quite surprised, and apologised before turning the lights back on.

Has anyone had a similar experience? Is it that easy to press the wrong button? It had never occurred to me just how dark it is down there!

▭ RichardP

Well, yes, exactly the same experience, a few years ago in that loooong gap in between Brisling (Highbury & Islington as pronounced by lazy drivers) and King's Cross on the Vic line. Tell you what, it seemed twice as long in the dark – no one moved, no one breathed – it was total silence as well as total dark. So dark I started seeing psychedelic patterns. It was an almost religious experience after years of London light pollution – the last time I was in the complete dark in fact. When we emerged into the station, the guy sitting next to me said 'wow, that was AMAZING!' Cue lots of passengers looking at me suspiciously like I'd been pleasuring him in the dark or something.

▭ Zed

Uniform

Whose idea was it to put some of the lovely LU staff in navy blue? They now all just blend into the crowds, making them nigh impossible to spot! Fingers crossed navy blue is on trial and not the new uniform! In an effort to be open-minded, perhaps navy was the old colour and the nice bright blue outfits are just at the cleaners?

💬 **Towerboy**

Sadly I think they are definitely here to stay. I overhead a couple of the gate monkeys at London Bridge discussing the new uniform and that they had to give their old ones back. They'll be issuing cloaking devices next...

💬 **Clefty**

Malaria

I am convinced that mosquitoes are breeding on the Underground. I fell asleep on my way home from one end of the Victoria line to the other last week, and by the time I got off I was covered in bites. Also there is a very strange insecticide smell in many tube stations. Very suspicious. So my question is this: can London Underground give you malaria?

💬 **Spotty David**

Spotty, you shouldn't worry unduly. There are probably mosquitoes on the tube, but they won't give you malaria. The most common form of mosquito on LU (and in London generally) is called Culex. Yeah, they bite, but don't harm –

you'll probably do more damage by scratching the bite.
They tend to live in pools of water, of which there are quite
a few on certain areas of the tube, owing to shafts, ducts etc.
LU's best bet, if they get infested, is to release bats (which
love mossies), although the bats will probably cause a whole
new set of problems!

💬 **robram**

Insecticide? You reckon? Bakerloo exit to Waterloo smells
of puke and feet.

💬 **phatflaresblack**

Even if there are mosquitoes down there, it doesn't mean
you're at risk from malaria. Ignoring the fact that mosquitos
are vectors (ie. transporting malaria from somewhere else),
only a few (one?) species of mosquitoes act as a vector
for malaria.

💬 **oops**

Malaria unlikely, fair David. But mosquitoes do breed fear.
Breed all the more in warmer times and need to feed on
blood. They can pass on any microbes, malaria or other,
that they have picked up whilst feeding. So those Victoria
line bites could have contained any virus that had passed
through on an infected human, or animal. Remember summer
'99, New York, when mosquito-borne West Nile virus swept
death and destruction through the city? TFL do, and so they
spray. We do, and so we walk or ride.

💬 **Galeria Gonnorea**

And just to feed the fear, we DO have the type of skeeter
in the UK that is capable of carrying WNV. We're also under
threat from the possibility of the mosquito that carries

Dengue Fever. If you think WNV is bit dodgy, dengue is a real stinker. Ooooh, stay in your homes armed with some really kick-ass carcinogenic insecticide. Might I suggest DDT, seeing as you're far more likely to get cancer anyway rather than a bloody mosquito-borne virus in the UK, FFS.

💬 Flo

Heat

The tube is vile today. I just need to get that off my chest. Turned up for work sweaty, greasy and nauseous and turned straight to TFL's website.
And you can imagine how pleased I was to learn that yes, it is acknowledged that in hot weather 'travelling can feel hot and uncomfortable'. And how delighted am I that they will be running another helpful poster campaign telling passengers to take a bottle of water with them on the train. And how outrageous that TFL ran a competition in hot hot hot 2003 to find an innovative and workable solution to heat on the tube BUT DIDN'T GIVE THE PRIZE MONEY TO ANYONE. Bet they used the £100k on the effing poster campaign. Bastards. Still, am looking forward to the arrival of the first 'air-cooled trains' in 2009. Only another four or five long hot vile commuting summers to go.

💬 stella

This is the very reason I have pretty much given up using the tube except when really pressed for time or it's pissing down with rain. I now walk from Charing Cross to Euston and back most days which is far nicer and gets me some modicum of exercise to boot.

💬 Riz

I realise it's not always practical but river transport in London is superb. I used to live near Canary Wharf pier and work at Blackfriars so the boat was ideal. It was a bit more expensive than the tube but boy was it worth it. Especially in summer when they used to serve drinks. Plus the fact they let season ticket holders on first. And one day I saw a porpoise in the Thames.

💬 **birdbrain**

Travel naked, spritzing yourself with iced water as you go. Where do I pick up my £100k?

💬 **part-timer**

Oyster

Am I the only person in London to be continuously hacked off at the fallibility of the Oyster card system? I get a monthly ticket (no Pay As You Go here) and use it on buses and trains, as well as tubes. However, I regularly have to suffer the ignominy of my ticket failing to be recognised by one of the readers at tube stations. It has nothing to do with the way I place my ticket on the reader and I have changed my ticket at least twice, because it has frustrated me so much.

When it fails, I have to wait for an LU member of staff to plod over and take my ticket from me, open it up carefully and lay it on the reader, only for it still not to register. I know waiting a couple of minutes extra isn't the end of the world, but Oyster cards were meant to speed things up at the ticket gates, not slow them down.

Do a certain percentage of these tickets fail to give LU staff things to do? Can anyone else sympathise with this never-ending predicament?

💬 **robram**

I've never had any trouble using mine in the zone for which I have a travelcard, but I have noticed that the new gates at Kings Cross never seem to work. Seems a bit pointless to spend money putting ticket gates up, only to have to let everyone through without checking their tickets as the gates are playing up... but then I guess that is LUL for you.

💬 **Salty McPepper**

Is it something in your wallet or pocket that's corrupting the card?

💬 **Nathan Barley**

I never have any trouble with mine. I've had it since they were first made available to non-LU people and it had a few glitches at the start one of which has left me with 9p spare on my card (or 1p missing, depending how you look at it). I keep meaning to ask them if they'll credit me the penny. My gripe is that the bus readers are so often broken and most of the time the driver hasn't even got the decency to tell you as you try over and over again to get it to work.

💬 **Mad King**

For starters it was only reluctantly that I got an Oyster card. I'm not impressed with having my life tracked in such a way only for the information to potentially fall into the wrong hands due to some inevitable but unforeseen security breach. The only thing that actually convinced me to get one is the dire state of the ticket machines on New Oxford Street, which seem to be consistently broken. About once a week I have to ring up the number on the machine to let them know it's broken again (why does no-one else seem to bother ringing, nor even informing other commuters I've been here so long now, yet I don't think I'll ever understand Londoners).

Anyway, my pay-as-you-go card was playing up a bit. I guess I have an honest face, and I'm always polite to those overworked and underpaid bus drivers, so this usually meant a free bus ride every now and then (although once I was told to get off and use the ticket machine at which point the driver just took off without me). That was until one driver suggested I try flexing the card a bit, so after a bend one way and t'other: snap! It broke clean in half. I sent it off with a form from a tube station about six months ago and haven't heard a peep from them back. I don't miss that card at all, but it'd be nice not to have to use those bloody machines again.

💬 pdr

Thanks for all the replies I'm glad I'm not the only one, and in fact, since posting, I've been getting more problems on the buses as well! However, in an effort to solve the problem I decided to get a new Oyster card but to my total lack of surprise the chap in the booth said: 'Sorry, mate, your ticket shows up on my reader, so you can't have a replacement!' I remonstrated with him for five minutes, before he reluctantly agreed to give me a form. Bizarrely, now after almost three months of frustration at not being able to sail through gates, my ticket has started working properly. Karma, perhaps?

💬 robram

If someone's got the bollocks to try and beat the system, i.e. not buy a ticket, then good luck to them. I'd understand if you somehow get busted by association but they are running the risk of the £10 fine or whatever it is. You are free to not buy a ticket and have a go yourself. But, like me, you probably 'prefer' to pay.

And, please, don't someone come back with something like by their not paying we all have to pay more. Utter bollocks. Something like 19,000,000 use the tube per annum so a few fare dodgers ain't gonna make the slightest bit of difference.

💬 Cotal Tunt

London by bus

Chirpy

Has anyone else had the pleasure of taking the number 38 to Hackney? The bus conductor is a most chirpy chap who plays the harmonica between taking people's fares. He's very accommodating on Tuesday I asked him to play the *Sesame Street* theme tune and he duly obliged. I don't know his name but he made my day.

💬 Louise

The harmonica man on the 38 is a quality bloke and is quite famous on the route. He released a single a few years ago which was advertised on loads of buses and randomly sponsored by Chupa Chup lollys if I remember rightly. Good to hear he's still around. I miss the 38, one of the best bus routes in London I reckon.

💬 Clefty

I too have had the pleasure of the harmonica-playing conductor on the no 38. This route seems to have lots of chirpy conductors, including the one that sings to everyone in rhyming couplets throughout the journey, the Irish conductor who will talk your ear off all the way to Hackney, the lady conductor who berates any man that won't give up his seat for a woman and the classic bus conductor who's 'been doing this for 20 years man and boy'. These characters always brighten my day and I'll miss them when the Routemasters go.

💬 **Hackney Girl**

Sounds like Duke Baysee – Arriva Buses had advertisements up on the 73 bus for his album for ages. Apparently he had a number one in South Africa.

💬 **Scott Keir**

My bus driver on the number 8 plays a trumpet fanfare when he arrives at Bethnal Green. Perhaps it is part of the new Transport For London ethos.

💬 **Louise M**

F.Y.I

Some tips from a bus driver:
- **Ticket machines: If they don't work the driver should take you to the next one and he's got to wait for you; his machine will not let him issue one so don't get shirty with him, if he did give you a ticket he can get in trouble.**
- **Bus stops: Please don't ask him to let you off other than at a bus stop, because although he might be doing you a favour, if seen by TFL**

or the police he can lose his license (yes it's that serious).

- The reasons why they don't stop: Bus is full, they can't overload or they will lose their license. If the bus stop says not in service they also don't have to stop. Bus drivers should always be patient and polite and answer your questions if they are able.
- Complaining: Ask for his badge number. If s/he won't give it you write down the route number, the direction s/he is travelling, the time you got on the bus and where you got on. Then when you get off, the plate at the side of the front door, which will be one, two or three digits long, and if it's possible the bus model number.
- Never complain to the garage; they look after their own. Complain to TFL on 020 7918 4300 and quote all the information and your complaint. If you get all the information they can discipline the driver while he is still on the bus.
- Black fingerless gloves: Almost every bus garage has got drivers who own these. They are very common. There may be more than one bad, rude driver out there...

⌨ north7

Top deck

Every day I use the bus route that goes up Clapham High Street to Stockwell tube. Most days I find that people along the route get on and stand in the lower deck area until it is crammed full. I always try to go upstairs, which is usually half empty. A couple of times I have called down the stairwell to tell people that there are seats available but they usually ignore me or look at me like I'm a mad crazy lady.

I guess people think it is not worth going upstairs as they are only travelling a few stops to Stockwell, but it drives me MAD! The point is, once the lower deck is full the driver won't stop to pick up more passengers along the rest of the route even though the upstairs deck is half empty. I look at the forlorn faces of the people at the bus stops we pass by and I think 'WHY WON'T PEOPLE JUST GO UPSTAIRS?'

Is this just a south London thing? Are Lambeth's school children so fierce that people are afraid to venture to the top deck? Why is it that people would happily lose an eye in the fight for a seat on the tube, but can't be bothered to climb some stairs on a bus? Is there a solution to this problem? Should I just ignore it? Or walk?

💬 Sqig (AKA mad crazy lady)

I can't speak for everyone/anyone else, but to answer Sqig's question on why I don't go to top of the bus, it is because I have a slight phobia of the top deck of a bus so prefer to stand even if cramped at the bottom. I too travel that same route, from Balham to Stockwell some mornings, and also wonder why other people don't go to the top, surely they don't all have the same phobia and fear of heights as I do?

💬 Wiesiee

The only explanation for this is that south Londoners, by nature, are extremely lazy. I used to try and get the 249 to Balham train station each morning from Tooting Bec but decided to give up after the umpteenth double decker went flying past my stop with practically nobody sitting upstairs. What I discovered was that people en masse were getting the same bus from the stop before mine to get to Tooting Bec tube. Obviously if they're too lazy to make the five-minute walk to the tube station they aren't going to make the five-second walk up the stairs to the top deck.

Surely the drivers should ask people to make their way upstairs if the bottom deck is full? It definitely seems to be a south London disease because the bus from East Finchley to Camden used to be a dream in comparison. Is this due to the number of hills in north London? Should there be a health initiative in south London asking people to climb more stairs? Who knows. All I know is it's bloody infuriating.

In saying this, bus drivers who have been driving half-empty buses have gone whizzing past me before with no excuses. Maybe it's my hairstyle they don't like, I dunno: they're a law unto themselves down here.

   ⌨ **That Bloody Scotsman**

No Squig, you're not alone; north Londoners are just as lazy. This kind of thing happens every day on the number 4 bus on my route in. That's of course the best thing about the soon-to-be-defunct Routemasters – at least the conductors could make the lazyarses downstairs go up. Keep shouting at the buggers don't worry if everyone else thinks you're mad. And while we're at it if there's a seat upstairs on the number 19 and the conductor is turning people off the bus telling them it's full, shout down and let them know. Yes, it's embarrassing, but you'll feel better for doing it the rest of the day.

   ⌨ **Highbury gal**

Sqig, I see this problem all the time on the 417 bus route, and, like you say, people couldn't get on the bus due to people refusing to go up stairs. My solution would be to get on the bus with a hot poker and see how they run! It's why I ride.

London by bike

Chavophobia

I cycle every morning from Dalston to the West End. This route takes me through the back streets of Islington and out onto Roseberry Avenue by Sadlers Wells. Islington has some of the worst examples of little, criminally-minded scumbags it has ever been my misfortune to meet. I've had rocks thrown at me, bags of chips, been mouthed-off at frequently. It's probably only the fact that I'm a fairly well built 6' that has stopped them trying to take my bike off me by force. As one kid said when I cycled past, 'If you'd been a bit smaller I'd have taken your bike innit.' A female friend going the same route got chased flat out by some kid recently, screaming at her, 'I'm having your fucking bike, I'm having your fucking bike!'

Born and brought up in Birmingham, I'm used to thieving little scumbags, but some of these kids are a breed apart, from the age of six onwards they're fearless career criminals.

The purpose of this rant? I'm applying for a job at the *Daily Mail*, this is a section from my covering letter. Either that or I'm making a direct plea for any retired members of the Brazilian police force circa 1979–1989 to come over to London and teach the Met the most effective way of dealing with child street scum. Alternatively, let's have a naming and 'shaming' of the areas to avoid for having the worst cases of mini-Chav scum. It's a public service. I nominate the entire area from the back of Angel along Essex Road as far as Newington Green. That's quite a big stretch and some bits of it look quite posh, and indeed are, I pity the suckers who pay through the nose to live in an area surrounded by sticky-fingered gremlins.

💬 **Dirtos**

Dirtos! As I read your post last week I wondered if perhaps you are not a doppelganger of mine. I also cycle from Dalston up Essex Road to the West End and am also 6'. But there is one crucial difference: apart from being told that mine was 'a nice bike' (I haven't locked my bike outside for more than a few minutes since), the little rascals seem to leave me alone. God knows I do my best to provoke them. One of them was idly circling Essex Road on a stolen bike one recent Saturday night and I had to apply my brakes to avoid hitting him. Non-bike riders may not understand, but essentially, braking to a cyclist is tantamount to pressing the red emergency open button on the doors of a bus: use only when stuck in gridlocked traffic. I was very angry. Naturally I inquired as to why he didn't steal some lights to go with 'his' bike. I find you can insult these boys with impunity because they will never catch you up. Either they don't have the lungs due to their smoking since the age of 0 or it may be the difficulty of pedalling a stolen adults' bike if you are only 10 years old and stunted.

💬 **Titus Goodlittle**

For really dangerous cycling in Islington, try the middle stretch of Caledonian Road (affectionately known as 'the Cally'), roughly adjacent to the Barnsbury 'conservation area'; those who require more of a challenge, try walking instead between the Ferodo Bridge and Cally pool, pausing for a while on the welcoming bench outside the *Islington Bar*. Scary shit, I'm telling you, with no bounds known to the variety of projectiles that will come hurtling towards you (ranging from spit, through stolen eggs, to seasonal explosives) accompanied by eloquent commentary and appraisals of your person from some of the most lexically challenged (pre-)teenagers of north London.

🗨 deefer

Lost

Has anyone noticed how expensive it is to retrieve your goods from lost property offices? I left a phone at a ticket office and realising my mistake just ten minutes later I returned. Too late. It had been sent to lost property. I then had to pay £10 to get it back, but because I had no way of proving it was mine, I had to spend half an hour describing the very specific screen saver (a turtle!) make, model, the first five names under 'A' etc. etc. He still didn't believe me even then, so I can only assume he enjoyed my company and the little game we were playing. It sure must be lonely in the depths of Waterloo lost and found. It's also cheaper to retrieve a cello...

🗨 Anon

Helmet

I cycle to work and I am amazed at how many people don't wear cycle helmets. Well worst-case scenario happened to me the other day and I was knocked off my bike by a car. All I can say is that I am very glad I had my helmet on. It would have been a lot worse as it saved me a bumped head! No matter if you think they look silly surely that is better that having a squashed head? PUT THEM ON!!!

⌨ injured

Oh dear, poor injured... Sorry to hear about that, I hope you get oodles of compensation (assuming the driver was at fault and insured!). Helmet vs bare head is a long-running and surprisingly bitter argument amongst cyclists. No doubt you know the arguments for wearing them, the arguments against go a little something like this (fingers crossed I don't get this wrong and provoke great ire):

1. They induce greater feelings of Invincibility in the wearer, leading to more risk taking and a higher incidence of accidents.

2. There's meant to be evidence showing they are more likely to cause rotational injuries (i.e. snapping your neck) in certain types of collision, where a bare-head would just get a bump or some grazing.

3. Forcing cyclists to wear them reinforces the mistaken belief amongst everyone that cycling is dangerous, when actually it is not, reducing takeup of cycling. (I certainly agree with this.)

4. Forcing kids to wear helmets also increases cost of ownership and means people are less likely to go get on a bike (see (3) as well), leading to a nation of lardy arses.

5. More pedestrians get serious head injuries every year than cyclists, but there's no campaign to make them wear helmets and you'd be laughed at if you suggested it.

I cycled in London for years and my cycling was certainly more… uh… adventurous when I was wearing my helmet. In fact I felt quite naked when I forgot it (which modified my behaviour). To be honest, if you really want to stay safe in London on a bike then lobby TFL so they don't let motorbikes and scooters use bus lanes; more cyclists die in collision with powered two-wheelers than with cars!

💬 **Konaboy**

Blimey – faced with such an outpouring of anti-helmet sentiment, I can't stifle an urge to make some claims on behalf of the other side. Half the argument against wearing helmets is a public health/public policy one about the effect of helmet-wearing on the popularity of the undoubtedly wonderful practice of cycling. But I, as well as all of you cycling LbLers, am planning to cycle on regardless of whether everyone else wears helmets or must wear helmets or anything else. So the question is: do the benefits of wearing a helmet *given that I'm going to cycle anyway*, and also given that I promise not to cycle less carefully when wearing it, outweigh the risks? There is no evidence, as far as I can tell, that they increase the likelihood of the dreaded rotational injuries – it's just that some doctors think that they might. And the lack of a drop in injuries as helmets become more widespread might be because of cyclists' rumoured propensity to ride more carelessly when behelmeted (a propensity I don't share, I don't think a crap polystyrene lid in London traffic doesn't make me feel invulnerable, trust me). I don't mind hitting my head on those few occasions when the bulbousness of my helmet is the reason that my head gets bruised. And apparently, if I fall off my bike onto a kerb, my helmet will save me. So what should *I* do?

💬 **Tomba**

Before complaining about motorcyclists in bus lanes, cyclists should fit mirrors, learn to check over their shoulders before changing direction and stop jumping red lights. I would be prepared to bet that this would reduce the number of collisions they have with motorbikes. Should I also mention the fact that cyclists don't pay road tax, generally do not have valid third-party insurance or any training?

💬 **Sam**

I recently got back into cycling after a seven-year break to compete in the London–Brighton (I recommend it). I don't cycle to work (no showers/secure parking at the office), but I did put in a lot of training on the streets of London. On each 30-mile training ride I do in town I've had at least one attempt made on my life by an errant driver. However, I've noticed cyclists are villains of the road too and there's a number of my kind who give the mode of transport a bad name. Since getting back on to two wheels, my top bothers from other cyclists are:

• Not obeying red traffic lights; hint, RED = ALL TRAFFIC STOP NOT JUST CARS! There are no excuses for jumping a

red light my friend got a £30 fine for doing just that on
his bike the other day... serves him right!
- Ignoring pedestrian crossings; as a pedestrian, imagine
how annoyed you get when cars jump them... don't jump
them as a cyclist.
- Cycling on pavements; THEY'RE FOR PEDESTRIANS...YOU
MUPPET!
- Not signalling; we all swear when cars don't indicate, but
you rarely see cyclists sticking their hands out.
- Not sticking to the left of the road (remember, you're
smaller than a car/bus/lorry and don't have its protective
metal skin!).
- Overtake on the right... not in the gutter on the left...
inbetween car doors and railings... silly... just plain silly!

Yes, drivers are pretty bad, but if we could cut out some
of the above, I'm sure our four-wheeled friends would
have far less to moan about... and could just concentrate
on perfecting the art of opening car doors without checking
their mirrors.

💬 **BC-The Cycling Geek**

I'm a cyclist, and I jump red lights. There, I said it. But I really
don't see anything wrong with it if they're approached with
caution and with eyes wide-open. Think about it — I'd be
allowed to jump off my bike and run across with it as a
pedestrian, which is slower, more cumbersome and possibly
more dangerous, but if I coast in and then cycle across
when I can see there are no cars coming the whole world
goes mad! Why? Jealousy? I can understand some cyclists
don't have proper awareness and so tarnish the image for
the rest of us, but it's pedestrians I find the worst culprits
for this; how many other of you cyclists out there have been

knocked off by pedestrians stepping off the street right into your path? I've been in London seven years, cycling all of them, and so far have been knocked off three times by pedestrians and never by a car. Anyway, back to the red light point – it's knackering cycling around, and if one thing pees me off it's getting some good momentum up and then having to stop at a pedestrian crossing because someone's pressed the button then crossed anyway so they're not even there I'm not stopping for that! Right, rant over; anyone agree with me or am I just plain wrong?

🗨 **Coningsby**

Coningsby – you said it all in just one line during your rant when you say you approach red lights open eyed checking for vehicles coming and then just go... does that mean you haven't looked on the pavement at the pedestrians who have now got the green man sign to 'go go go'... think about it! Oh and all those cyclists who don't wear a helmet, my friend lost her dad in a very tragic accident involving him on a bike and a car door being opened... he flipped over the top and landed on his head. He wasn't wearing a helmet and is now brain-damaged! Be warned, these accidents may be quite rare, but they do happen... it's better to be safe than sorry!

🗨 **V**

To redress the balance: Sam, a high proportion of London cyclists are members of the LCC or even the CTC. So they do have insurance. And I, like many other cyclists, pay exactly the same amount of road tax as you do. Because I also own a car. I'm probably a better road user than you because I have a bit more tolerance. So don't mention it, pipe down instead.

Cycling Geek, for someone who has only been riding since June you are very opinionated. I suggest you open your horizons and travel abroad. Perhaps you could visit one of those advanced countries where even cars can proceed for a nearside turn (often right but would be left over here) whilst the light is on red. If the road is clear then there is nothing wrong with proceeding on a red light. If the way is not clear then you are a prat and will get knocked off. I think it is the car driver in you that is getting wound up there. Chill out. You might also want to take some advanced cycling lessons as your road positioning appears to be wrong. Cyclists are not required to give way to cars, buses and lorries.

🗨 **absolutechaos**

If you want to mandate any safety item, glasses are the first thing to buy. It's not just to look cool, but dark glasses in good weather reduce light (obviously), but even clear glasses at night are vital so as to stop air streaming into your eyes. Even a sedate 10–12 mph is a fair wind to be shoving London's dirt into your eyes. I'll continue to not wear my helmet thanks, although I'm happy that you're concerned for my well being.

PS. While we're dishing out intra-cyclist advice and knowledge, here's a request. Obey the rules of the road. There is *nothing* I dislike more than seeing fellow cyclists going through red lights and riding on pavements. It's unnecessary and it only inflames drivers' tempers to make life more dangerous for the rest of us.

🗨 **loaf**

In response to loaf's P.S. thank God there are still cyclists around who get annoyed with other cyclists who jump red lights. I walk an hour each way to work every day and have lost count of the number of near misses I've had when crossing at pedestrian and zebra crossings, where cyclists keep going even when the rest of the traffic has stopped!

🗩 **Beeg**

Loaf says there is nothing he hates more than seeing fellow London cyclists jumping red lights and mounting pavements. Well for me one of the joys of cycling is that we don't need to slavishly follow the rules of the road. Stay safe, yes, but wait at a red light on a pelican crossing when there is no one walking across you've got to be joking!

🗩 **Bill**

In response to 'Bill', who writes '...one of the joys of cycling is that we don't need to slavishly follow the rules of the road...', my wife was knocked down by a prat like you on a bicycle, on one of those pedestrian crossings you dismiss so readily. He went through a red traffic light. She was wheeling our six-month old son in his pushchair. Luckily she only broke her shoulder in two places, but at least the cyclist got to carry on enjoying the 'joys of cycling', eh. You idiot.

🗩 **Jase**

London by cab

Angels

I can't count the number of times I've missed my last train at London Bridge (sort it out Southern trains!) but last Sunday I found myself in the familiar surroundings of the taxi rank at London Bridge station. It was late, we were freezing, and as usual there was a long queue and no cabs.

Then, suddenly, a cab turned up, and the woman next in the queue opened the door, then looked over at us and shouted 'anyone else for Brockley?' We were travelling to Forest Hill (minutes from Brockley) so said 'Yes please!'

Has anyone ever experienced this kind of generosity anywhere before, let alone in London?! I am still amazed to this day! We thanked the taxi angel many many times, and she said 'it just makes sense doesn't it?' Wowee.

I shall definitely do the same in future (as long as I'm not alone, but then I guess she was happy to share with a lovely looking couple like me and my fella).

Come on London share the taxi love!

💬 **Gob-smacked**

I think sharing taxis may be common only to those in SE London. I have done the same at London Bridge and, perhaps even more surprisingly, have always found people in the taxi queue at Lewisham willing to share cabs. You have to be a bit trusting before you jump in a cab with someone going to your home address though, but I would always try it in a big queue – so much cheaper to share and safer maybe than night buses.

💬 Emma

I am gobsmacked myself that (a) this has never happened to you before (terrible place, this London!) and (b) you have never done it yourself! (How many poor people have you left in the cold?) I do this all the time and have been since uni when I was poor and needed someone to share a fare with. I even got a job out of it once! I was queuing in a rank trying to get to an interview, when my taxi came I offered the rest of the queue the option to travel to my destination. A guy jumped in and by the time we jumped out I had gotten myself another interview which turned into a job! Brilliant!

Next time, just think about how nice and warm the gesture made you feel and don't worry about the unfriendly people staring at you like you have a tin of beans on your head – more fool them! Oh yes, and be careful doing this at night time and never do it on your own in a minicab!

💬 Big Sis

Ranking

Has anyone else been to the cinema at the Barbican on a Sunday evening to see absolutely loads of taxi cabs parked on the single yellow lines around there? What are they doing there?

💬 Griff

It's a taxi rank.

💬 Miss Moneypenny

No it isn't. If it was, it would be a two mile long one, wrapping itself around numerous buildings in the general Barbican area. If you don't know, shut up.

💬 Griff

On balance, I think that taxis queueing outside the Barbican on a Sunday night probably *does* constitute a taxi rank. There's usually a concert or something going on in the main hall and, with a capacity of 2000, I'd have thought at least a few people might want a cab?

💬 Stocky

I'm not sure exactly where the line of cabs near Barbican is that you're talking about, but a friend of mine used to work for the big law firm Linklaters (their office is behind the Barbican). They always had a long line of cabs outside their building, which I think were meant for all the lawyers who worked so late through the night that they had to take cabs home.

💬 Pop C

Hail

Does anyone know under what circumstances a black cab with its 'For Hire' sign illuminated can refuse a fare? I've heard that they're not allowed to refuse a fare if the destination is within six miles of Charing Cross, but is this true? Can they refuse you if you are carrying drink/food/too much shopping, or just don't like the look of you? And what should you do if they do refuse to stop/accept your fare? (I was surprised to find out that until last year they weren't allowed to refuse you just because you were smoking.) I've emailed the Carriage Office via the TFL website, but so far no reply...

💬 Tim

If it's within three miles they are meant to stop but they don't. We were refused a lift by a black cab apparently because my boyfriend was wearing his bag in a strange manner (I suspect it was actually because we didn't live on the cabbie's way home). The new tactic is all about subterfuge. Pretend you're going east, even if you're not, and if you're just back from holiday, cunningly hide your suitcase.

Apparently cabbies don't like to pick up people with luggage outside tubes because they know there's only a short fare in it for them. And for you cabbies who object to what I've just written, stick it up your minicab. Where were you last Saturday at 3am when I was tired and emotional in London's West End?

💬 minicab

A black cab driver cannot refuse (without reasonable excuse) any fare within six miles of Charing Cross (or 20 miles for Heathrow). What constitutes 'reasonable excuse' is any one's guess, but it would have to be something acceptable like:

- being drunk
- refusing to pay a deposit (where a deposit would be reasonable)
- attempting to carry a load or cargo of an unreasonable nature, e.g. a big dog, anything dirty or dangerous (you'll have to think of something yourself on this one)

- having a contagious disease
- attempting to convey more people than the cab is licensed to carry.

He (or she) cannot refuse you because you have shopping bags or luggage, neither can they refuse to carry you because of your appearance unless your appearance gives cause for other concerns. However, if you do complain to the Public Carriage Office it will come down to being a situation of your word against the cab driver's, unless you have other proof. The PCO however does take all complaints against cab drivers seriously, so do not be put off from making a complaint if you feel you have been genuinely treated badly by a London Cabbie.

Ninety-nine percent of London Cabbies are decent hard working guys and girls, but please don't start quoting the Hackney Carriage Act 1843 to them, because most of them know it well enough to offer an informed reply. Ultimately, at the end of the day, a London Cabbie is self-employed and if he or she doesn't want to carry you then let them suffer the loss and take another cab.

💬 **Bakerloo BadBoy**

Having lived in London for a number of years now I've sampled both black and mini cabs when travelling about. Recently a friend gave me the number for Addison Lee and they have been fantastic so far.

The cars are all new and are often minivans and they charge by postcode to postcode. For example Bethnal Green (E2) to Kennington Lane is £11 whilst in a black or minicab you are looking at £15! If you are really clever and the place that you're going to is on a postcode border then getting dropped off a little bit earlier can save you more money! For example E2 to Albert Embankment near MI5 is only £9, saving £2 on getting to Kennington Lane or £6 on going a little bit further round the Vauxhall one-way system! I work at a club called Fire in Vauxhall, which is in SW8, and it costs £15 via Addison Lee and more in a black cab/minicab, but if I get dropped off on Albert Embankment then it's £9 and Kennington Lane £11 bargain or what?

☐ RichBowen

In response to Bakerloo Boy's comment that 'a London Cabbie is self-employed and if he or she doesn't want to carry you then let them suffer the loss and take another cab' – the day that this attitude is recognised as an integral part of the 'women get raped by minicabs' problem, we may finally start to put closure to these attacks. The refusal of black cabs to pick up women at night is the *primary* cause of us taking unlicensed cabs! Thanks for the clarity on cabbie laws, and I will be quoting *and* snapping licenses with my camera phone when refused!

☐ Jannani

It is interesting to read the usual slagging off of London taxi drivers. Just a few points you might be interested in:

1. The number of people applying to do the knowledge (student taxi drivers) is now at an all-time low. So low that the Public Carriage Office has reduced the minimum age to apply to enter the knowlege to 18 (yes 18 years old!). It appears that the PCO is as much in touch with the industry it licences as the people who write on the *Evening 'SubStandard'/Daily Mail* why-o-why/etc.

2. The average age of a London taxi driver is 55. So there you are. In a few years' time, there will be no problems with taxi drivers because there will not be any just like plumbers/electricians/carpenters etc.

💬 **Satisfied?**

If your correspondent Jannani is that concerned about taxi drivers, maybe she should become one and practise what she writes. (Providing she is over 18...)

💬 **Tim**

Really? I never seem to have problems finding plumbers. Why, *Yellow Pages* has loads of yellow pages devoted to them. While we're on the subject, if the driver of cab number 13489 who I hailed in the snow in Baker Street last night is reading, I'd love him to explain this exchange...

ME: 'Crouch End please mate.'

HIM: 'Hmmmmm... no.'

ME: 'Oh. Why not?'

HIM: 'Well, I thought I was stopping for that fare up the street.'

ME: 'I just asked her if she wanted to go in this cab in front of me, and she said "no, you take it".'

HIM: 'Well, it's not up to her.

ME: Well, sorry but seeing as I'm here anyway, please can you take me up to Crouch End?'

HIM: 'No.'

ME: 'Why not – aren't you free?'

HIM: 'I don't have to take you anywhere.'

ME: 'But your light was on, so I thought you did – what sort of cab are you?'

HIM (DRIVING OFF): 'No.'

ME: 'I'll take your number and report you then, if that's OK?'

HIM: 'Do what you fucking like...'

Or he can go fuck himself. I'm easy.

⌑ **ils**

In response to Tim (what a nice guy – not!) I have to say that, as a lone female, I've had several black cabs screech off into the dark foggy night when I've asked to be deposited at my house in N1! Not a nice thing to happen and well within the alleged five-mile radius. When I've discussed it with the next cab to come along, they all express horror at their fellow-cab driver that's 'let them down' and told me to 'bloody well report the buggers'. One cab that stopped had actually seen the previous cab high-tail it out of there and couldn't actually believe it when I told him my destination; 'That close?'

Unbelievable response from Tim... does that mean that whenever we receive bad service we should take the job over? Can we never complain about rudeness? Or potential danger? Get a life – or better still... try flagging down a cab to go home wearing a skirt and heels and see how successful he can be.

PS. Can he tell us where he's getting his stats? I'm a doubter...

⌑ **Deb the regular cab-user**

Just to add to the debate about taxi drivers, I would like to say thank you to an amazing cab driver called Richard who found my phone in the back of his cab, took the time to trace me and then brought the phone to me when he'd finished for the day. It restored my faith in cab drivers and Londoners!

⌑ **Zogs**

My father is a cab driver. He's a grumpy git some of the time, but he's a good cab driver. He drives people to where they want to go and he too is appalled by my tales of being refused by black cabs. However, he also has to put up with a lot of rudeness by passengers. He's had fares run off without paying and his cab is broken into repeatedly (although he never ever leaves any valuables in there) and has to deal with the repairs the break-ins cause. There are always those who give any profession a bad name, but there are those who take their jobs and responsibilities seriously. Report those that don't do what they are supposed to but don't tar all cab drivers with the same brush.

💬 mappeal

Bendy

Has anyone had amusing experiences on the new Bendy 73s? I was on my way to Angel from Stoke Newington on Saturday and the driver actually got off the bus somewhere a little way down Albion Road, screaming, 'I'm having a nightmare! I don't want to hit it! My heart is beating so fast!' Poor guy! How much training did the drivers actually get before they were let loose with those 18-metre monsters I wonder? That said, I usually travel on two wheels and getting rid of the Routemasters means that you don't get pedestrians jumping off in front of you without looking.

💬 Liner

London by bus

Cockle-warming

Okay, after all this public-transport slating I have a story that will warm the cockles of your heart. Last week I had the pleasure of taking the 185 from Lewisham and getting off just before Forest Hill. As I got off there was a very doddery old man doing his best to make it to the bus stop in time, but despite his best efforts was a clear 20 feet away after everyone had got off the bus.

He had his hand out indicating to the driver that he wanted to get on, but behind me I heard the bus doors close; same old story I thought – if you're not at the stop you can't get on and nothing on this earth would make the bus driver wait. But no, I turned round to see the bus pull out, trundle 20 feet along the road, stop, open the doors and scoop the old man up. Such a rare occurrence, it genuinely brought a tear to my eye. More nice stories please!

💬 Sam

Well, I don't know much more about London than many locals, but having lived in the north-west of town for 16 months, I have discovered how rude bus drivers actually are and Sam's experience is quite rare. However, as a 'converted' Northerner (this city is tops and your transport system is actually very good), I do have to comment how much more friendly Northerners really are. Sam's tear-jerking moment is an everyday occurrence 'up North'. So come on you bus drivers, have a heart!

💬 Becksy boy

Another heart-warming experience on a bus in south London: a woman disembarking the 468 called a friendly 'Thank you' to the driver, who swiftly responded with 'You're welcome!' I was so delighted with this unusual kindness of words in the great metropolis, but I'm afraid I couldn't bring myself to do the same when I left. Imagine the wonderful effect if we all started thanking our bus drivers!

⌐ **RichP**

You mean to say that you don't already?! If I get off at the front door of a bus, I always make an effort to say thanks/cheers just as I step off. I'd do the same at the central door if the driver could hear me too, in which case if I am walking in the direction that the bus is facing, I will nod and/or smile at the driver to say thanks instead. Why on earth couldn't you manage those words yourself? Are you polite-o-phobic or something?

⌐ **Dave**

I used to live in Glasgow and it would have been the height of bad manners to get off the bus without thanking the driver. Now, I recognise that where the off door is miles from the driver this is hard, but wouldn't it be nice if we tried to improve London by thanking drivers when they've got us from A to B safely and comfortably? After all, it must be rotten dealing with customers' rudeness all day.

⌐ **Superali**

Please don't start pretending that all bus drivers deserve thanks for their driving, some drivers should be apologising to me when I exit the bus. I'm not 'polite-o-phobic' but I am scared by the reckless and inconsiderate way some of the

bus drivers get along their route, maybe 'thoughtless&
impolitedriver-o-phobic' would be better!

I agree if the journey had been pleasant and helpful
than thanks should be given but when the driver has
raced off quickly giving me no chance to reach my seat,
missed my stop so I've had to walk back 400 metres or
accelerated and braked too hard so I've nearly fallen into
someone's lap then I consider that to be the 'height of
bad manners'.

True, it must be rotten dealing with customers' rudeness
all day but when the drivers show no consideration for me
it is all too easy to react with rudeness. I think if they
drove a little more considerately and were more thoughtful
of people on their bus then they would receive a lot less
rudeness and a lot more thanks.

⌨ Ginger Badboy

Naughty

I have recently found two ticket machines at a
South Eastern station which are behaving 'oddly'.
If you dial up a return ticket from Zone 3 into
the City at 9.20, it'll cost you £4.70. But at 9.21,
you can buy a cheap day return, for £2.60.
Now, the miserable old witch who works in the
ticket office won't sell you a cheap day ticket for
the 9.24 train. She won't sell you one of those till
after half past nine. So the moral is, kids? If you
have to get a train, like me, between 9.21 and
9.30 in the morning, try the ticket machine first
and see if you can save yourself a couple of quid
every day.

(I'd rather not tell you which station it is, in case something is done about it, but the combination of 'Zone 3' and 'miserable old witch' narrows it down.)

💬 Thomas the Tanked Up Engine

And finally

Free?

While at my barbers the other day, having one of those sociable chats with the fellow punters, an ex-tube driver explained this. If, at the end of the day, the barriers at a station allow you through but you miss the last train, the station is obliged to pay you for a cab home. This is obviously something London Transport would never advertise but is this true or complete tosh? Seems very generous (and completely open to abuse) to me.

💬 Minesapint

It's kind of true... London Underground will pay for your taxis if you miss your last tube due to a late connection, but, and here's the rub, only if you are a lone female. I was taken from Baker Street to West Hampstead in a taxi courtesy of LU about a year ago and the staff were lovely. It was such a nice surprise to not have to wait for a night bus on a freezing winter evening.

💬 Riesie Mittens

I have the definitive answer on this now from my
brother who works for LU. The last train time is always
advertised on a white board at every Underground station.
If for some reason the final train is taken out of service
without notice, then London Underground is obliged to
pay for every person (not just lonely females) to continue
their journey. This will not mean a cab all the way back
to your front door, but to the nearest tube station where
trains are still running, or the closest tube station to where
you live. However, my brother (and many of his colleagues)
will try and assist anyone who is genuinely stranded to
get home. Please don't take the piss though – this isn't
a LU service – he and his colleagues kindly fund your
journey home out of their own pockets if they believe
you are genuinely in distress or stranded, and it is amazing
how many 'genuine' cases never bother to come and find
him the next day to repay the cab fair home (less than
half in fact).

Most (of course not all) station staff are genuinely
kind people, so please remember that next time you shout
at them for taking your train out of service (normally because
someone has puked up in a carriage and they don't want
you sitting in it). Apologies for the rant, he is my little
brother so I can't help sticking up for him!

💬 TK

Places

In many ways, London is like a great big *piñata*, and everyone who lives here is like an excited, blindfolded child with a heart full of hope and a big flailing stick. Aim that stick right and London will split at the seams like a ruptured spleen, showering you with the most extraordinary places to visit, places like you won't find anywhere else in the world. Get it wrong and the chances are you'll lose your  footing and end up in a frustrated, eyeless heap. In this section, we take the guesswork out of your donkey-bashing and tell you the best places to picnic, to park your car, to get married, to find London's Latinos, to find tomorrow's papers and so very much more...

London by where?

Croo shon

Has anyone got any good euphemisms that estate agents supposedly use for parts of London that they want to make sound posher than they are? I can think of Crouch End being pronounced 'Croo-shon' in a French accent, and Streatham Hill being dubbed St Reatham's Hill, which I suppose is some kind of rare genius. (Or is that people who live in these places want to make it sound that that they are far more desirable than they are? Either way.)

🗨 Tiddles

When we were looking for a flat, we noticed a lot of the estate agents' windows boasting beautiful flats in 'Harringay Heights'. Yes, it's on a hill. But everyone knows this is the car-filled ugly Wightman Road connecting Finsbury Park to Turnpike Lane. It's Haringey for God's sake, and I can't imagine anyone would be fooled. (I have lived there, by the way, and quite liked it... but it is ugly).

🗨 Tash

As a current denizen of Croo Shon, I can confirm that it is just like *fin de siecle* Paris... a hotbed of radical thinking, crammed with sizzling Symbolists, but still a trifle more Rambo than Rimbaud at chucking-out time. However, I was once taken to see a flat that an estate agent assured me was in North Kensington; I thought our final destination of Harlesden was stretching that definition somewhat...

🗨 ils

Not exactly a play on the name, more being geographically
'misleading'... South Chelsea for Brixton. There is actually
a South Chelsea school of English just across from Brixton
tube. Hmmmm.

◻ **The Beak**

Lord, there are loads of these, and some have been going
round for aeons. Here are some the ones I remember;
Clapham – Clay-fam; New Cross – Nouveaux Croix; New Cross
– Gate Portillon De Nouveaux Croix; Battersea – Bat-TER-ze-a;
Elephant & Castle – south-central London; Limehouse –
Limehouse Village; Staines – St Aines on Thames; Brixton –
Briton round the Cross.

◻ **Wooden Horse**

I can remember a time when some obviously very stupid
refugees from Fulham began referring to Cla-am (Clapham),
Bat-ay-sia (Battersea) and, of course, Ba-alm (Balham).
However, the Northcote Road area of Bat-ay-sia, just south
of Cla-am Junction is known as 'Twixt The Commons'.
These days it appears to be more about displacement;
for example, almost anywhere north of Tooting Bec is now
Wandsworth Common, whereas the part of Wandsworth
Town near the river is Putney.

I've even heard Pimlico referred to as 'south Belgravia'.
The only thing you can be certain of is that an estate agent
will never use a correct name if there's the opportunity to
employ something more pompous.

◻ **auawsha**

County

With all this talk about Middlesex and Surrey and whatnot, it reminds me of an Easter chat I had with an Aussie mate (I say this so we can both be excused for not knowing)... Is London a county?
I never know what to put when I'm filling in forms, and usually I just leave the 'county' field blank. But I have heard that London used to be (mostly) in Middlesex. Hannah mentions that the London County Council was formed in 1889 but I've never heard of it, I guess it changed into the Greater London Authority or whatever Ken's mob is called. So is it officially a county or what?

💬 **Brendan**

Until 1889 'London' was just the City of London – what we now know as the 'square mile' and was governed by the Corporation of London. Everything else we now know as London was a collection of small villages and settlements known as parishes (with the exception of the City of Westminster). These areas came under control of four counties: Middlesex – everything north of the Thames and west of the River Lea; Surrey – everything south of the Thames and to the west of New Cross; Kent – everything south of the Thames and East of New Cross; and Essex – everything North of the Thames and West of the River Lea. The City of London was self-governing and was not part of any county.

In 1889, in response to growing urbanisation and problems that the essentially rural parishes and county councils were not equipped to cope with, the London County Council was formed, this now governed everything we now know as inner London (e.g. Westminster, Islington, Camden, Hackney, Tower Hamlets, Kensington and Chelsea, Hammersmith and Fulham, Southwark, Lambeth, Lewisham, Greenwich and Wandsworth). Below this tier the parishes were formed into metropolitan boroughs, which were smaller than the current ones (generally two metropolitan boroughs make up a current London borough). The outer London areas were still controlled by the Middlesex, Kent, Surrey and Essex County Councils.

In 1965, as outer London became more urbanised, the London and Middlesex County Councils were abolished and the Greater London Council was formed. More urbanised parts of Essex, Kent and Surrey were also added (i.e. Bromley, Dagenham etc.) and the old metropolitan boroughs were merged to form the boroughs we know today. London then ceased to be a county.

In 1986 the GLC was abolished by Thatcher and London had no government above the boroughs (with the exception of bodies such as London Transport etc.). The GLA (Ken's lot!) are not a replacement for the GLC as their role is more strategic and cannot influence the government of London as much as the old GLC did. Through out all of this the City of London has remained independent and self-governing and has never been part of a county or larger governing organisation (except HM government!)

So today London is not part of any county or indeed any type of coherent city; it's essentially two small cities and a collection of boroughs – it's surprising we ever get anything done!

A rather long essay I know but I hope that clears a few things up!

                                               💬 **Hannah**

Hannah's essay on London made fascinating reading
(more please!). But it did confirm something I and many
people are beginning to think: London is just too big.
I think the outer boroughs should return to the counties
they came from. That is Bexley to Kent, Croydon to Surrey,
and Middlesex to be brought back to life. This would give
people a greater sense of being part of something and not
this gigantic mismatch called London.

💬 **Dick Wittington**

A very full answer from Hannah but it didn't answer what
to put on those annoying web forms when it says county
and there's a star next to it which means you have to
put something. I always end up putting London again,
which looks really dumb as the parcel is then addressed
to London London.

💬 **Crouch Ender**

Sorry if I'm wrong, Dick W, but those boroughs that
Hannah referred to don't mean that the places you
mentioned are part of London. Croydon is very much
still a part of Surrey and has been for a long while.
Equally Bexley (while governed by Bromley Borough) is
also classified as Kent. Bromley itself is very much a Kent
conurbation, rather than a London suburb. I imagine those
people who live in both Bexley and Croydon would be a little
upset to be classed as Londoners. There's a fine line between
what is and isn't London, but in this case those places are
definitely NOT London.

💬 **robram**

Missing link

On the full tube map the Northern and Bakerloo lines both stop at Charing Cross. I myself have changed from one line to the other at this station. In individual line maps for the Bakerloo and Northern lines that you see above your heads when on the tube, it shows NO London Underground connections at Charing Cross! Why is this? Why do they not want people to know they can change at Charing Cross between the Bakerloo and Northern lines? What is their dark secret?

☐ SuperFlake

It's to save your feet, I would imagine. Charing Cross tube station used to be two separate stations (the Bakerloo line end was called Trafalgar Square, the Northern line was most recently called Strand, but was also called Charing Cross and various other things) and were only connected when the Jubilee line was built (note for newer Londoners: the Jubilee line used to terminate at Charing Cross). Because of this history, there is a very long walk between the Bakerloo and Northern line platforms. It is far quicker and easier to change between the two lines at Embankment or Waterloo, where the walk is much shorter. So not a dark secret, more LUL trying to be nice.

☐ Jif

Area code

Bit geeky but has anyone else noticed that Beckton in east London (right at the end of the DLR) is in the 0207 telephone area? This seems a bit strange as I would have thought somewhere like Whitechapel would have been the eastern extremities of the 0207 area. Anyone out there who can explain this anomaly?

Elton Stoney

Those with short memories might have forgotten how controlled the media used to be under the Tories, but when the Canary Wharf development was being launched and we were being told it was the future of London, the small matter of it being 'well east' with no roads was addressed by simply strong-arming BT into giving the whole area an 01 code (now 0207).

piehead

Not sure how Piehead managed to turn a question about Docklands phone numbers into a rant against the Tories but it would be helpful if he took his red-tinted specs off for a minute and looked at the facts.
1. 01 numbers used to go out as far as Dagenham so Beckton has historically been well within the London '01' range.
2. The reason it won 071 status (now 0207 via 0171) rather than 081 status was due to the fact the planned Docklands development was primarily seen as an extension of the CBD (Central Business District).

The primary redevelopment pitch was commercial with residential coming once the commercial development had been embedded. The LDDC lobbied BT of this obvious fact and won their case. And the wealth-creating glory that is now the London Docklands area can thank such far-sightedness for its success.

💬 **Leftie-nonsense-corrector**

There is a little bit of nonsense in Leftie-nonsense-corrector's own posting about Docklands. If s/he thinks that Beckton is anywhere near the CBD-extension that is the Docklands development (or more correctly, the development in the immediate vicinity of Canary Wharf and now Canada Water tube), s/he needs to take a long hard squint at a map.

What piehead said about Docklands being a white elephant was largely true. It is only in very recent years that Docklands again, Canary Wharf has become a (relatively) bustling area. Canary Wharf is certainly not the 'wealth-creating glory' that s/he purports it to be. Despite this resurgence following the promise of the '80s and the fallow years thereafter, much of the Docklands area remains desolate. It is a rather sterile and superficial environment not assisted by its proximity to the Thames, making for most uncomfortable journeys in the autumn and winter due to the biting winds.

I have worked in the West End, the City and in Docklands before the bomb went off outside our building, destroying it and taking two lives. (For the uninitiated, this was not the Canary Wharf bomb, which is how it was billed by the press, partly because everyone has heard of it, but also because the *Mirror* and *Telegraph* were ensconced in their ivory tower there and could make themselves look awfully brave by continuing to work. Not that they were threatened

by the bomb, nor suffered anything more than increased
security and a few delayed DLR trains, but that is
another story.)

Anyway, Docklands a success? Well, occupancy rates are
up, there is a feeling of a lively working community and
there are a few better bars and restaurants (I remember
when the highlight of the year was the opening of the
Tesco Metro in Canary Wharf). But a success? Not yet,
at any rate. Transport could still be better a river service
would be useful. But it is the feel of the place I dislike.
There is something particularly unpleasant about the place,
and a kind of feeling that more 'sensitive' types pick up in
horror films in the passages before it becomes apparent
that the hotel they are staying in has been built over an
old burial ground.

While a community is undoubtedly developing it feels
more like The Village and I am 'No 6'. I and many colleagues
avoid going there for meetings, simply to avoid the dreary
architecture and planning, excessive thrusting corporate
iconography, not to forget the awful microclimate.

🗩 **psaf**

I hate to be a pedant, and it's at a complete tangent to
the discussion, but actually there's only one London area
code (020) – the local numbers for London now consist
of eight figures and just happen to start with a 7 or 8,
depending on which area they were in before BT
consolidated the numbers. So we're all one happy
family and can put aside our bourgeois pretensions
about dialling codes and Tory conspiracy theories
about docklands.

🗩 **fluffy mark**

Hospital

In the transport section of the first LbL book, there is a message from Tizzy which mentions Chelsea and Westminster Hospital and no one knowing where it is...

I started work at Hammersmith Hospital which is next to the Chelsea and Westminster Hospital in Acton. I have also had to visit Charing Cross Hospital in Hammersmith... How do the hospitals get their names? Why not rename them all to the area they're in? And why are hospitals not listed in the A to Z? It makes life very difficult...

💬 Chanted_snicker

Are you sure you've seen the Chelsea and Westminster Hospital in Acton? When I (as a nurse) last did a patient transfer there it was in Fulham. I agree with you about Charing Cross Hospital though – hugely confusing and no idea why!

💬 lofty

To put an end to the confusion about the Charing Cross Hospital is called so... because it used to be in Charing Cross! Yes really, it's that simple. Most inner-London hospitals were moved further out when it was realised that the population of London didn't want ill people nearby, or they were bombed out in WWII, or land in the centre of town could be put to more profitable use. If you are interested in London's hospitals, workhouses and asylums (and who isn't?) it's worth paying a trip to London

Metropolitan Archives in Clerkenwell where they keep the records of most London hospitals (including some very interesting but desperately sad photo albums of inmates from Victorian lunatic asylums): www.cityoflondon.gov.uk/lma. Actually, LMA is a great place full stop if you are at all curious about London history and the staff are fantastic and very helpful (I used to be one of them!).

💬 Hannah

Suffering by London

The awful tooth

I knew it would start eventually. I have been putting off visiting the dentist ever since I left home to go to university. Does anyone know of a good, cheap, gentle patient-focused dentist, preferably in the SW areas of London? Who is not going to charge a small fortune for 12 years' worth tooth decay?

💬 Scared and Broke

I'd recommend the *Earlsfield Dental Centre*. It is private so not particularly cheap but, unlike some of the cowboys out there, they don't invent problems to treat. I've been there a couple of times now and if all you need is for them to count your teeth to check they're all still there, that's all you get.

💬 Sophie

I can recommend *NHS Dentist* in Fulham. They only
deal with NHS patients, so aren't trying to persuade you
to have really expensive treatment rather than the cheaper
NHS alternative. They were busy, but very thorough and
professional. I had quite a lot of work done so the
course of treatment lasted for three visits. Including an
appointment with the hygienist it cost me about £90.

💬 **Less Gappy Than Before**

I can recommend the *Dental Clinique* in Balham
(www.dentalzone.co.uk, 40 Balham High Road, 020 8675
7307), no hassle getting an appointment if you're NHS
and they treat private and NHS patients. I needed some
work done and they weren't pushy to get me to have the
most expensive treatment.

💬 **Suj**

If you're looking for an excellent dentist in the centre of
town there's this place called *Dental Spa* on Charlotte
Street just north of Soho, they have all the latest kit
and can do a crown for you in one visit (none of those
two week waits with a temporary tooth). Best of all, they
have two massage/beauty treatment rooms and a solarium.
They have a website, which is www.dental-spa.co.uk.

💬 **jcrw**

Pain

My boyfriend seems to be allergic to going to
the doctor, and flits between chronic backache
and a very odd burping problem (what a catch eh?!)
Now, girls, you'll back me up on this one, but there
is only SO much sympathy a girl can offer their man

particularly when he doesn't want to go to the doctors to get any better! Am at the end of my tether here – can anyone recommend or advise on alternative medicine in west London? Acupuncture, nutritionist? I have no idea where to start.

💬 Popsickle

I too hate the doctors (more because I can't be arsed to sign up than genuine fear). I got a really painful back problem from sitting hunched over my desk all day and was generally miserable for ages. Eventually I went to see a lovely lady called Alison Durant who is a registered osteopath and she sorted me out quick sharp, no weird waiting rooms, no mindless forms, no mental doctors receptionists to deal with. I'm now slightly less hunched and much, much happier. Contact her through the *Ladbroke Rooms*, W10 5SH, 020 8960 0846, or *Holmes Place* gym in Notting Hill. Good luck with the burping; at least it's not farting.

💬 Spaniel

Popsickle, I can only recommend not wasting your money on alternative medicine. However, alternative medicine practitioners are often more sympathetic and caring than GPs (you're paying by the hour remember) so your boyfriend may be more inclined to visit. Try someone who doesn't rely on quackery, like a massage therapist – just make sure they massage his back not his 'aura'! And remember, people always seek help when pain is worst, so it will inevitably improve immediately after treatment. The acid test is if the symptoms are relieved in the longer term.

💬 once bitten

Popsickle, I sympathise. However, there are many things that can be done about your boyfriend's hot air problem. Those of a delicate disposition may want to skip the next bit. The backache is probably due to trapped wind and this eases when he burps (yuk) so the back ache goes away. I suppose you have tried the obvious things such as asking your pharmacist to recommend something for trapped wind. Other little things that might help are drinking peppermint tea after every meal. Also, drinking less beer (he'd probably prefer to see a doctor if he's anything like my boyfriend). Taking short walks a couple of times a day will also help shift the air more quickly (or sitting at desk, he should twist ankles round so feet rotate). One treatment that I thoroughly recommend is reflexology; this is where pressure points in the hands and feet are pressed with the fingers. Each point corresponds to a different part of the body. People have been known get instant results as far as digestive troubles are concerned (you do not want to know the details...!). Although I am not able to recommend somewhere to have the treatment done (I do my own and also have the luxury of a fully trained mumbo jumbo Mum who looks after my well-being for me), reflexology treatments are available everywhere these days – beauty salons, chiropodists, alternative therapy centres, gyms. Usually they range between £35 and £60 per treatment. If it works, you can buy a book and then self-help at home. I am a much healthier bunny all round for reflexology. Hope that helps.

⌐⌐ **Hocus Pocus**

Done?

I've just moved to London, near Park Royal tube, NW10. I'm paying £600 pcm excluding bills, am I being done?

🗨 bongo the clown

I reckon it much depends on what kind of accommodation you've got. Beautiful views, period features, designer homeware, free toiletries, chocolates on pillow? Or room and use of kitchenette/shower-room, dodging the floorspace piled high with friendly Antipodeans? We (a couple) rent a spacious one-bedroom flat in great condition with stupendous views (we can see the Wembley arch) in leafy nearby Ealing for £800 pcm excl. bills. (Admittedly the decor is rather seventies bordello, but free fireworks displays all October and November make up for it.)

Since Park Royal, or at least the bits I've seen, is not particularly leafy, I'd think you could get something cheaper, unless it's me who's got an unusually good deal. In which case, I am drawn to the far-from-unusual conclusion that LONDON COSTS TOO MUCH! On the other hand, a pal of mine rents a room in an ex-council flat in Southfields for £450 pcm excl. bills but no gch, just electric heaters, and not at all in good condition. And another pal rents a very nice one-bed flat with her partner in Finchley for £910 pcm incl. water and half council tax. Good luck negotiating.

🗨 longterm renta

Living by London

Plaistow?

We're thinking of moving to Plaistow. We've found a lovely flat there but the area seems a bit, um, rough. As two single girls, should we be worried? And is there actually *anything* to do there?'

💬 **Kate**

Don't move to Plaistow. It's horrible, there's nothing to do, nothing to see. It looks rough because it is rough. There's absolutely nothing to recommend it. I got mugged at knifepoint within a month of moving there.

💬 **PeteFromPlaistow**

Plaistow is brimming with fun and exciting things for two young ladies to do on a Friday night – first avoid the brawling at the Greengate pub, then a bit of pool or snooker at the salubrious pool hall and finish off this fun fest with a loverly kebab on the way home (dodging the joy-riders of course). Lest I forget, there is also the Balaam Street swimming baths where they throw in floating plasters and verrucas at no extra cost. If you are determined to stay east, then I would say that Leytonstone or Stratford would be a better option!

💬 **teepot**

I don't technically live in Plaistow; I've got an E15 postcode but I'm a stone's throw away. Well, it's certainly not Islington or Clapham. There aren't many (any) nice restaurants, coffee shops etc. But I've always felt safe because it's usually pretty busy, my neighbours are proper east London down to earth, and most importantly the average person can afford to have a nice flat/house (which is why most of us are there instead of living in a dump or shoe box just to be near a 'nice' area!). I've got lots of friends dotted around east London, and for some reason we're all pretty loyal and fiercely defensive of the area. Lots of money is being pumped into Newham and I reckon it feels upbeat. And depending on where in Plaistow it's very good for transport links, very easy to get into town or Docklands for when you do feel like being in a less 'rough' area. But if you need a starmucks coffee every morning and want an *All Bar One* as your local move along please...

💬 **Plaistow Plasterer**

For anyone who remembers it, I believe the Levi 501s ad that featured a guy smuggling jeans through a Russian airport and back to his miserable apartment block in Moscow was actually filmed in Plaistow, it having the appropriate Soviet architecture. On the other hand, when I lived in E15 the local pubs would put little plates of nibbles out on the bar (sausages, cockles, cheese etc.) on a Sunday lunchtime for everyone to snack on. So Plaistow might be an ugly place, but at least you don't get chiselled for bar snacks.

💬 **vincentwong**

Battersea

Apparently Battersea Power Station is going to become the centre of a large shopping, leisure, conference and accommodation complex, due to open in 2009. Well, hurrah. I've been hoping somebody could come up with a use for the place. Not that a 'shopping, leisure, conference and accommodation complex' is the greatest thing in the world, but it surely beats an abandoned, crumbling ruin that's only used as a heliport.

💬 Robo

A 'shopping, leisure, conference and accommodation complex'? Jesus. Like we need another one of these. Endless strip-lit corridors meeting at cod-Italian piazzas with tinkling fountains, lined with branches of *Gap*, *Footlocker* and *Boots*. Meanwhile, yuppies swoosh about their trendy offices on the top floor on hover-scooters, before heading up to the exclusive riverside roof terrace to sip Jacob's Creek and laugh annoyingly. Give me a crumbling power station any day.

💬 Tiddles

China down?

Was half-listening to the news the other evening and half heard a story about development in Chinatown. Something about tearing down the existing buildings, including the Pagoda (!!) and replacing everything with a *Tesco* supermarket or something equally bland.

Does anyone know anything about this? My gut reaction to this is: bejesus! More corporate blandness eroding the cultural diversity that makes London such an exhilarating city. But as I said, I was only half-listening and I don't want to go off half-cocked until I know more. So if anyone has any details, please do divulge...

ZeroGravitas

I saw the same story as ZeroGravitas about the proposed levelling of Chinatown, and I'm overjoyed. The streets smell of rotting food and the pavements are covered with that weird grease. The area reeks of decay and needs cleaning up. New and hygienic doesn't have to be corporate and bland. Why are Londoners so sentimental about squalor? If this was any other country, Chinatown would have been cleaned up long ago.

fluffy mark

According to a friend of a friend of my neighbour's dog, Chinatown is a tad worried at the moment because the landlord who owns most of it has put up the rent by around 400%. And not all the restaurants (certainly not el cheapo and el crappo buffet) are willing to pay that.

badly dubbed boy

Fluffy mark, methinks your observations would be true of most of London. It is one of the dirtiest cities I've lived in around the world, and I've lived in a few. But, by gum, I still love this place! Which makes me wonder, why the hell do we put up with this filth? Why is it completely acceptable for people to drop their detritus in the streets, and on the buses, tubes and trains? And why, oh why, is it acceptable for people to spit everywhere? I do believe humans possess a swallowing reflex but Londoners seem to be evolving without one...

ZeroGravitas

This is not a response about Chinatown but a response on ZeroGravitas' mail about the filth in London. I totally agree. There is crap everywhere and I think it's the worst aspect of London. I'd suggest that we employ FAR more street cleaners, or instead of handing out ASBOs to little gits, give them a good dose of old-fashioned Community Service with 100% of it being street cleaning.

FilthBuster

I hear you on the litter and spitting front ZeroGravitas. I've taken to attempting to shame people into picking up their litter. It really gets my goat to see people just dropping stuff on the floor, especially when they're all of about two paces from a bin. Lazy fuckers. So I pick it up and either hand it to them or put in the bin to demonstrate how simple it can be. Not all the time, but when the mood takes me (and I have judged the offender unlikely to assail me with a knife or some such unpleasantness – this isn't actually a cause I'd die for). If you're in the mood for a bit of self-righteousness I thoroughly recommend it!

Magpie

I totally agree with ZeroGravitas that London is far dirtier than it needs to be. New York, Paris, Barcelona – all big but far less minging so what's our excuse? I'm beginning to think Londoners actually like it this way it; feeds this idea that we're all edgy urban warriors, clambering over sacks of rubbish, old kebabs and dog shit, all whilst clutching an overpriced latte and an iPod. It also seems no one wants to speak out about the sheer volume of scary-ass junkies hobbling round Bloomsbury/Camden etc. for fear of being labelled a right-wing nut who wants to cart them all off in a truck, Giuliani-style. Believe me, there is nothing 'urban' or 'edgy' about being mugged or hurled abuse at in your lunch hour, it's just horrible...

💬 **Salty**

Latin

Does anyone know of any of the places where London's growing Latin population hang out? I am not looking for a cheesy overdone salsa joint, just a place to go and hang with Latin people and absorb some Latin culture, any ideas?

💬 **Desperately Seeking Some Latin**

London's growing Latin population hangs out at the Elephant & Castle! There's a lively contingent who've taken over the upper floor of the shopping centre and a variety of new businesses on the western side of the roundabout, including a small complex of stalls in the old post office and a club called *The Ministry of Salsa*.

💬 **ninorc**

Try Galicia, a restaurant and non-stop hang-out for Latin types, on Portobello Road. Also on Portobello between the Golbourne and Kens Park Road there is the *Spanish School* and a bunch of other Spanish businesses with loads of Latins hanging out around and in them.

💬 Jannani

Stockwell has a thriving Portuguese community and the main road (Stockwell Road) has a string of Portuguese restaurants and cafes, and there is a branch of *Lisboa* there for groceries and bakery stuff.

💬 AJH

The Latin community has seen big increases in the Elephant & Castle/Walworth Road area in south London over the last couple of years, hence the big street parade that happens every year in August, 'Carnival De Pueblo', which just gets bigger and better. However, at other times of the year you can 'hang out' at, wait for it, *The Ministry of Salsa* on the Elephant & Castle roundabout. Surely it doesn't get better than that eh?

💬 X marks the spot

In love & skint

Okay I know this question probably highlights lack of imagination on my part. But I have gone to restaurants, cinema, the *London Eye* and even a few shows in London with my girlfriend. What other new and exciting things can I do in London with her? I have just finished uni so things are very tight but I still want to have a good time with her when we go out. Any IDEAS?

⌐▢ **Bad bwoy**

Get yourself a book of London walks; good way of seeing loads of bits of London you miss whilst walking round on a daily basis and won't cost you a penny, apart from the pub lunch at the end. There are organised daily walks too check out http://london.walks.com. If you are planning on taking the summer off then it might be worth thinking about doing the Thames Path. This starts at the Thames Barrier and finishes 180 miles later at the source in Gloucestershire.

⌐▢ **Cazza**

One of the nicest things that a boyfriend ever did for me was to take me to *London Zoo*. It's not cheap, but you can spend the whole day there, and take a picnic. The *British Museum* is great as well (and free), just pick the bits you want to see before you go and get a map, otherwise you can get a bit overwhelmed by what is there. What else...? Well all the free museums and galleries, obviously (*Tate, Natural History Museum, Museum of London, V&A* etc. etc.), the botanical garden on top of the Barbican Theatre is worth a look, punk/goth spotting in Camden Town, watching street performers in Covent Garden... In fact, how could you POSSIBLY run out of inspiration in London?!

⌐▢ **Good Girl**

Crumbs bad bwoy... where to start? Try one of the late
views at the big museums, the *V&A's* is on Wednesday
nights until about 10.00pm, free to get in, there's a bar in
the entrance, usually a DJ or some live music and you
can wander around the galleries without the usual crush.
I'm not a huge fan of traipsing around museums or galleries,
but it has to be one of the most spectacular bar locations
in London.

💬 **Kensal Green**

The London open house weekend in September is
always £3.75 well spent. Buy the guide at
www.londonopenhouse.org and then spend the
weekend getting in free to houses all over London that
you wouldn't normally be allowed in. The houses range
from grand Crown Estate buildings to architects and keen
DIYers who own swanky pads. We had a very entertaining
time visiting one of the 'dancing' houses near St Pancras
who took us on a tour of their school interspersed with
performances of contemporary dance (although I don't
think they found our uncontrollable fits of childish giggling
as amusing as we found their silent 'getting buggered
up against a wall and swinging round a lampost' dance).

💬 **Harri**

Have a look at *LondonFreeList* (www.londonfreelist.com)
it 'lists all the events and attractions in London that you
don't need much money to go to. They are all either free
or cost no more than £3 maximum.'

💬 **Abi**

Picnic

We're planning a huge family picnic mid-August as an informal 'baby welcoming' for our daughter. Which park should we choose, and how do we check that the date doesn't clash with some huge event like 'Party in the Park' and the like?'

💬 mommy

Why not try Greenwich Park, it is huge and has lots of different areas a deer park, a kids' boating pond and duck pond, children's playground, and of course the *Royal Observatory* and the Meridian Line. And great expanses of grass to sit on for your picnic and trees if you need them for shade. And lots more. As far as I am aware there are no concerts planned in August. It's also easy to get to Greenwich; even though it's in SE London we have DLR, trains, or come by boat from any of the central London piers. Have fun!

💬 olhol

A fantastic park to have a picnic in is Richmond Park, there are ponds, streams, woods, ducks, rare birds, some facilities (generally near the various car parks), a golf course and deer. Loads of them! It's a very natural place, not manicured gardens and the like, rugged, hilly, flat and very grassy. If you decide to go for Richmond Park, follow the signs to Pen Ponds for two gorgeous big ponds with loads of ducks and geese to feed. Might not be the best place to picnic but is a gorgeous sight.

💬 peelit

Epping Forest is a beauty for summer country picnics,
at the end of the Central line and is closer than you think.
It's good if you take a bike with you though, as Epping Forest
is MASSIVE. There is also Ham (Richmond) by the river,
which is where I used to go as a kid, I went back there
recently and it is still lovely. You can paddle in the Thames
when the tide comes in and in late summer there are
blackberry bushes to be found! Don't tell everyone though
this is my secret Enid Blyton dreamland.

🗩 Clefty

Take the tube to Cockfosters and explore Trent Park.
It's a nice country park with walks, muntjac deer, picnic
areas etc. In the centre, you can observe students in the
wild as Middlesex University has a campus there. Hadley
Wood and Monken Hadley Common are also worth exploring.
You can walk from Cockfosters or take the overground to
Hadley Wood.

🗩 billy

Challenge

I am a big fan of London, having lived both in Islington
and Clapham for the past two years. My long-time,
long-distance partner is shortly going to move in with
me; however, only on one condition: that we escape
the madness and live in a quiet and green area (of London),
or else leave the city in favour of a smaller town/village.

Now, I very much want to stay in London, but the greenest I
have seen are the big central parks and commons where you
can still hear the encircling traffic noises, planes flying overhead etc. I need to find a part of London that encourages the

illusion of a quiet, safe, small-town community.
A neighbourhood where you can ideally hop on a bike and within minutes be cycling in what seems like 'proper', undisturbed nature. All this, while at the same time being connected and central enough for me to get to work at London Bridge as well as the West End for fun at the weekends.

It's quite the challenge, but can anyone recommend areas of London that meet these conditions? Much obliged...

💬 **Lupe**

Ahh... you see Lupe, you're on the wrong side of the river. If you were to travel a few stops down from London Bridge, you'd find leafy Camberwell/Peckham/East Dulwich/Nunhead. East Dulwich has all the Hampstead-style farty shops; Peckham has the inner city grit; and Camberwell has enormous tree-lined avenues and rather good bars along Camberwell Church Street. Nunhead has lots of little green bits, including a funky Victorian cemetery and the legendary Peckham Rye. Good bars and eateries are thin on the ground, but it's getting better.

💬 **Sladey**

I do like a challenge! I would suggest that Hampstead (although pricey) has all of the necessary requirements for you and your long-term beau. It's on the Northern line (perfect for London Bridge and the West End) and is in Zone 2, so not *too* far out to feel like you're not in London anymore. There are some fabulous shops, restaurants and bars, and of course Hampstead Heath so that you can both get your greenery fix! The streets are very leafy and lovely and to me, it just seems to have a feel-good factor there...

💬 **Blonde Chick**

If you want green space but still near good connections, move to Greenwich/Blackheath. It has the biggest park, but which, unlike Clapham Common, isn't covered in dog poo. Has train connections to London Bridge/Charing Cross/Victoria and has a lovely cosmopolitan atmosphere. I moved over from Clapham and can't believe I didn't do it sooner. Oh and also there's loads of good pubs.

💭 Cherub

Have you ever been to Beckenham? It's got a lovely villagey feel to it and is on the edge of south-east London for those bike trips into Kent, but it's only about 20 minutes on the train to Victoria or London Bridge. I should think you and your boyfriend would be very happy setting up nest there. Good luck!

💭 fluffy mark

In response to Lupe, I too love London and this passion for my city has increased even more so since moving to Primrose Hill, which, incidentally, I believe may be the answer to your problems. I don't know what your budget is, as it is rather expensive unfortunately (hence why I live in a room the size of a box, almost). But if your priorities are: 'quiet and green', yet still central, you can't go wrong. Location, location, location. It is like a tranquil haven in the midst of a metropolis, and has a 'village atmosphere'. Not only do you have the hill with some of the best views in London, but also Regents Park is literally just down the road for yet more greenery. Not only that, but it is very near Chalk Farm, so very handy for getting to London Bridge and the West End. Added bonus, you get all this peace and quiet, yet it is still in

Zone 2. By the way, the only noise I generally hear in Primrose Hill is people mowing their lawns and doing DIY, so quite suburban really (in the best possible way, of course). Although Chalk Farm is close by, it is kind of separated by a bridge. PH is its own enclave really. In addition to all the above, PH has some of the best pubs, cafes and restaurants, and excellent transport links to other hidden gems in London. Highgate, Hampstead, Belsize Park and other nearby north London suburbs are also supposed to resemble a village, but I can't recommend Primrose Hill enough. Good luck convincing your partner! I'm sure they will love you, and London, forever once they see Primrose Hill... P.S. it doesn't really do it enough justice, but see www.primrosehill.com.

💬 **Lucky Layla**

What about Walthamstow? This is the first area I've lived in during my many years in the capital where my neighbours came and introduced themselves. Our house looks out over a park, transport into town is quick via the Victoria line, and it's still in Zone 3. Just a very short cycle ride away is Epping Forest. The only thing that's missing is a cinema, but hopefully that will be rectified soon.

💬 **strawberryfluff**

Park

Reading some RAC survey about jobs and parking I had a bright(ish) idea, I think: don't know how many people on LbL have cars as London dwellers, but imagine some do. Why not pool our parking knowledge? Where are the best, most hidden or cunning places to get a parking spot in areas of the capital? Will the Sinners and Winners man watch it for you whilst you nip across the road? Answers on a postcard please. (As an aside, if anyone is looking for some fairly secure parking in Brixton I've got a space I don't need at the moment.)

⌨ **Mr Ben**

Chambers Road and the surrounding streets behind Holloway prison – park to your heart's content for free.

⌨ **belisha beacon**

Do you know how difficult it is for local residents that surround Chambers Road to get parked without you blabbing your mouth off? Obviously not! Because non-residents use this 'free service' and there isn't enough room for local residents they are now going to introduce Permit Parking. So, now I'm going to have the privilege of paying to park near my flat along with the inconvenience of the council putting the bloody things in!

So, a big thank you to all the non-residential parkers who are going to give me the opportunity to spend my money on something else that used to cost me nothing. And a very special thank you to belisha (big mouth) beacon for letting everybody who didn't know in on the 'secret'.

⌨ **Grumpy Old Man**

Siblings

I have just made contact with my long-lost brother who was put up for adoption before I was born. We've arranged to meet up next week and I'm very excited. However, throughout all of my excitement I'm coming up with a blank for a nice place for us to go and have a chat. We were going to go to *London Zoo* but it turns out that it's my brother's 'special place' with his girlfriend. I don't want to change any memories they have of that place.

I'm thinking the obvious such as *Tate Modern* as it'll give us a chance to walk and chat in relative peace, but I'd like to be able to take him to somewhere really special that will give us a chance to get to know each other as we have a lot of catching up to do. I'd like to get some personal recommendations so I can make the day really special.

Newly Found Sister

I think the *British Museum* and the lovely new space covered by the amazing glass roof might be a nice place to go to walk and talk. Lots of places to stop and chat and only tourists to overhear stuff you might be talking about. In the warm and lots of interesting things to jog the conversation if it goes quiet – best of luck...

smoothcheeks

I would just like to wish Newly Found Sister the best of luck meeting her brother for the first time. I have a sister who was put up for adoption and she found us too and it was brilliant to meet her and get to know her. It is so strange and wonderful when you start to find out all the madly similar things you do and say! I would recommend a walk in Richmond Park as it is beautiful in Autumn and will give you time to speak to each other and of course say hi to the deer. Followed by lunch or dinner at *The Roebuck* at the top of Richmond Hill, this would make a good and easy day out. Really good luck and I hope you enjoy a great relationship with your new brother as I do with my new big sister!

💬 Clairey

Boring

Having just moved offices from Moorgate to Spitalfields I want to invent two awards with the following nominations:

1. **London's Most Beautiful Building. This just has to be Christ Church Spitalfields. The way it looms over the whole area and glares down Brushfield Street with such proprietary authority – what a fantastic monument to Hawksmoor.**

2. **London's Most Boring Street. This has to be Moorgate because things get more interesting whatever direction you go in. East and it's the buzz of Liverpool Street/Spitalfields. West and you're in Smithfield. South and at least it's the City proper and north gets you to bohemian Old Street. Moorgate, meanwhile, has M&S and a branch of *Lewins*.**

💬 Office Mover

Wedlock by London

Wed

I'm due to be getting married in London next year and I'm struggling to find a good venue. I don't want anything too stuffy or formal and ideally something with lots of personality (that can hold a lot of people, ideally 150) and that allows you to let your hair down and have a good old fashioned knees-up. Any suggestions?

💬 **Maud**

One of my work colleagues got married in the RA (Royal Academy) building just off the strand last summer. They've got a great cellar space for dancing and drinking.

💬 **Anon**

For a venue that is really quite flexible and can be what you want to make it, can I suggest *Westminster Boating Base*? They have a reasonably large function-type room overlooking the river, with three glass walls and balcony that they hire out for weddings and parties. They hold 150 seated, up to 350 buffet. You can also take pleasure in knowing that the costs go to keeping the boating base (a charity) running to allow cheap sailing and kayaking for children.
See www.westminsterboatingbase.org for details.

💬 **elaina**

I got married in London in February, at the *Commonwealth Club* on Northumberland Avenue: www.rcsint.org/club. It may be a members' club but it's not stuffy; it's all very modern and the staff are great, so helpful. We had somewhere between 150 and 200 people, and took our own DJ and band. The venue hire and food are pricey but I'd thoroughly recommend it. The food is to die for; and the venue hire cost covers unlimited tea lights, flowers on the tables, menus and place cards (lots of venues charge extra for all of these). Depends on what sort of budget you've got. I would also recommend these websites as a way to find venues: www.fluidfoundation.com/venues.asp; www.citybash.com. I've used both of them in the past and they come up with some interesting ideas, lots of places I've never heard of before. We almost got married at the Battersea Barge. Only reason we didn't was because it was a bit of a trek from the church. It's quirky but fun, and a lot cheaper than the place we did use!

💬 **braindead geordie**

I got married in 2001 at *The Royal Chace Hotel* in Enfield, in the pavilion. The main reason why we chose it was that it's very relaxed and they do a barbecue for lunch! (It's shown in the picture on the right on their homepage: www.royal-chace.com.)

On a summer's day all the patio doors are left open, they have chairs and tables outside, a lovely lawn complete with its own fountain, and the pavilion has its own dedicated bar. We even got a bouncy castle for all our friends' kids to play on during the day which meant with the children well occupied, our friends could relax too!

The staff are great and very helpful but they don't get in the way at all – everything simply 'works'. Your party is pretty much left to its own devices and we had a great time – it's the ideal location if you want somewhere where everyone can chill out, and just enjoy themselves. Plus at the end of the evening everyone can migrate into the hotel bar for drinks as late as you like (and then promptly fall into your hotel room afterwards!).

The only disadvantage for you could be that it's not in central London, but for me, where all my friends live in north London, it was ideal! I can't recommend the place more highly!

💬 **samsid**

I'm getting married in August and as London is more expensive than anywhere else anyway and given that as soon as you say 'wedding' to any prospective venue, they can't see for the pound signs in their eyes, we chose to get out of London, hire a field, marquee, generator, do a pig-roast, do our own bar (booze-cruise), get in our own drugs and not have to worry about anyone's licence or transport home because we're all camping in our field.

Granted, the majority of brides-to-be would consider that just a little too close to roughing-it. Weird eh?

💬 **olly**

Hen

I'm getting married in August and want to have my hen night in this great city of ours. Any suggestions of any different group activities and venues suitable for a party of about 15? Google's just sending me down the usual tacky strippers and L-plates route, and I'm after something a bit more civilised.

☐ Pixie

My friend took over this ceramic café for her hen where they give you paints and you decorate plain white china plates, cups etc. and we all painted her an expresso cup and saucer, then they were glazed and fired and now she has a set to remind her of us. They let us bring our own booze in so the artistic results were interesting, to say the least. Then we went up the river on a boat cruise and drank more champagne, then out for tapas. It was all very civilised and fun.

☐ Badger Kitten

I had a lovely hen weekend recently. We rented out the lovely *Peek House* in the Rousden Estate on the south coast near Axminster at around £125 each for 13 of us. The place had seven bedrooms (some double beds, some twins, five or six of them en suite) a massive dining room, cinema room, games room, spa treatment room with a lady who would come in and give you massages and stuff, and a private beach, although it was a bit of a muddy trek to get there.

We thoroughly enjoyed ourselves and were hugely impressed by how nice the house was. Great if you want something relaxed and a bit more civilised. Might cost a bit more in peak season though and may well have had something to do with the head bridesmaid's razor-sharp negotiating skills!

kaymonster

Look out for promotions that the big stores put on. I started off my hen weekend at Harvey Nics, we'd managed to get tickets through the *Sunday Times*, and basically we got a goody bag full of gorgeous stuff (Dr Haushka, Ren, Mac, and lots more) plus free manicures, eyebrow pluckings, makeovers, massages and champagne. Then we went to Brixton and did a pole-dancing class which was a wicked warm up for the big night out. Try www.polepeople.co.uk. They provide cocktails to make you feel less inhibited.

   Myhotel in Chelsea also does a great 'Girls night in' package where the bride gets an upgrade to the Thai suite. Think you even get your own butler, girlie vids and lots of booze. Otherwise an animal-loving mate of mine is starting hers off at *London Zoo*…

kit

How about going to *Jongleurs* comedy club, it's a fab night out and they've got quite a few locations, the best thing about it is you eat, drink and all from the comfort of your seat. Then you can boogie the night away after the comics finish. They cater for big groups too.

Crofty

Stag

I am getting married next summer and hope to have my stag night/weekend in the only city worth celebrating it in. However, as with all major nights out, the possibilities in London are overwhelming. Google only really throws up the clichés.

Not being a massive outdoor crazy sports type, I'm toying with making it a sophisticated (but still fairly cheap!) affair and wonder if anyone has hired anywhere that will provide you with a private casino-type feel for the night – a cards room with bar etc? I wonder if any other LbLers have been on unusual, fun or rarefied stag nights in our fair capital? Any ideas welcome.

RP

This might be a tad corny now, but a few years ago I was best man for a stag do in London, and went down the Monopoly pub crawl route. Sixteen lads, two hired limos (doesn't cost that much split between a load of people), and an 11am meet in Waterloo station, ready for the trip out to Old Kent Road.

One of the limos died outside Kings Cross station, so we got a healthy refund and let the other limo go. We did the rest of the crawl in black cabs, which isn't as expensive as you might think. It may have been cheaper to do the whole thing in cabs, but the limos did make life easier while they lasted. Incidentally, we didn't make it. If I remember correctly (which, for obvious reasons, is a fairly tricky thing to do), we managed 20 out of 26 locations.

Mike

Our work Christmas party had a casino theme. It was held at the *Connaught Rooms* on Great Queen Street (above Sway Bar) where we were treated to a pretty good '20s-style jazz band, and they'd set up roulette and blackjack tables for us. Of course the gambling was not for real money we were each given fake money at the start of the night.

💬 Pete R

Shopping by London

Trendification

Is anyone else as appalled as I am by the changes at the *John Lewis* department store on Oxford Street? My sister and I used to have a theory that if you couldn't find what you wanted at *John Lewis*, you probably didn't need it in the first place. Now, however, our little theory is being blown out of the water by the 'trendifying' changes that have taken place. They no longer sell cleaning materials when they used to have the best selection of any shop I'd ever been to. The glove department has been reduced to a couple of those mini-carousel displays when there used to be rows of a wide variety of gloves available. These are the only changes I've noticed so far, but I'm guessing that there are others.

Why? Why have they changed what was (in my opinion) the best department store in London. It wasn't highly fashionable, but it was reliable, dependable and it reminded me of being taken there when I was little.

I'd like to do a flash mobbing of the place with everyone wearing black armbands to show how much we mourn the loss of what was an institution. Or am I the only mourner?

🗨 **mappeal**

I am similarly dismayed by the trendifying of JL on Oxford Street. I read an article about it and apparently post-congestion charge they weren't getting as much business as well as fighting off stiff competition from *House of Fraser* and *Debenhams*. I think cleaning materials are still in the back left-hand corner of the still fantastic and recently expanded kitchen department in the basement. Long live haberdashers.

🗨 **Guilty Emma**

What are you going on about? *John Lewis* selling loads of gloves and cleaning products? I'd imagine the demand for loads of gloves and cleaning products really wasn't there. As for flash mobbing – that's so last year. I'd imagine there are better causes to wear black bands for. My advice get out more.

🗨 **Dr Spewan**

I agree! The haberdashery and associated craft/material departments are a shadow of their former selves, and material has even moved upstairs. Instead the men's clothing department has moved up from the basement. There are lots of men's clothing shops around but only one *John Lewis* haberdashery department, and now that's better at *Liberty*!

I also miss the 'atrium effect' which used to go up the centre of the store and the hat department is smaller... There is nothing so cheering up as going to try hats on.

💬 **grumpy not so old woman**

I too mourn the demise of *John Lewis* and its own legendary capability to store everything under the sun you can't get anywhere else. A year or so ago, I stood, alone, on the 1st floor with my jaw almost stuck to the floor, in disbelief and horror. The haberdashery department was a shadow of its former self. No longer the reams of fabric, no longer the pages and pages of dressmaking patterns, no longer the little extra decorations to sew or trim your lovingly created scarecrow fashions. Reduced to a box of safety pins. It's a tragedy! I'll join your flash mobbing! Where and when?!

💬 **Tubeworm**

John Lewis on Oxford Street has undergone a massive facelift but I am pleased to confirm they still have a fab selection of cleaning products in the basement. Last weekend I noticed at least four or five different types of red wine stain removers plus all the usual cleaning stuff. Once you get past the new trendy bits it is the same old *John Lewis* underneath and still my favourite department store!

💬 **jennyliz**

Papers

One of the little delights of London is being able to buy the next day's paper in the evening (save for the recent unhappy London news)... where exactly can you do this now, and any idea from what times, on what days? I can't find out online and I can see a handy LbL Guide coming on!

☐ TonyW

Being able to pick up Sunday papers on the way home after a Saturday night out was one of the nicest things I discovered when I first moved to London. They sell them outside lots of tube stations I think, including Elephant & Castle, Brixton, Stockwell and Leicester Square.

☐ MM

There's always a large newspaper stand outside Leicester Square station's corner of hell (you know the one under the Hippodrome) in the wee hours; always found this cheering, that other people were just starting their day when mine was winding down.

☐ Alastair

Read the comment by TonyW yesterday and whilst walking home happened upon a stall selling today's papers at just after 10pm last night. Figure this is pretty much what he was looking for! There's a man standing just east of the Marble Arch Entrance to Marble Arch tube, on the north side of Oxford street. Try there!

☐ Toby

Juicy

I used to buy my Sunday papers late on Saturday
night at Liverpool Street, just in front of the
fruit/veg stand which is located in front of the
tube entrance turnstiles. I haven't done this
for a while now, but I hope it is still possible;
there is something ridiculously delightful about
being one step ahead of the early Sunday
paper readers.

💬 Ronnie

Not if you're Jude Law there isn't. If one of the
tabs has a big story, the first editions don't
contain the really juicy stories as they don't
want their stories poached by the other papers.
As the cocksure Mr Law discovered to his cost
when the *Sunday Mirror* held their revelations
about him and that nanny over to later editions.
Mr Law had checked the first editions and
went to bed believing that his liaison remained
secret. Not to do with London, I grant you,
but funny all the same.

💬 Linda Palermo

Funky

I have been searching for years (but not too hard to be honest) to find cool, funky, warm slippers. I don't want any of those old-looking grandpa-type slippers that are oh so boring. I would like to get hold of Spitting Image characters or cartoon characters on my slippers. I've seen them, so I know they exist. The idea to get the feelers out was sparked when I went into a shop with a mate and said I'm looking for a cool pair of slippers, he said he's been looking for years, I said I don't believe it, he said yeah, honest. So in case there are others out there like him and I, are there any shops in London that someone can recommend that sells cool, funky, warm slippers?

Ben

The only funky slippers I've ever seen are made by Skandium – home of cool Scandinavian furniture and homeware that (bizarrely) also produces a range of felt slippers. Check out the 'Miscellaneous' section of their products on their website (www.skandium.com). You can buy them at the Skandium store and also in their concession down the bottom of Selfridges.

Brooce

I found the best slippers in the world in a strange gadget shop in Wan Chai station, Hong Kong. Sadly, after a search round the flat I can't for the life of me find the bloody bag. However, on inspecting the slippers themselves I found a tag that said they were made by

'Milk Design' along with a quote from Confucious:
'The wise are active, the virtuous are tranquil'.
Slippers with a message... you can't go better
than that!

⌐ **Clefty**

You have to go and check out the *O2 Centre* on
Finchley Road for slippers. My husband dragged me there
over the weekend and I was sold! As you come in the
entrance from the main road look right. There is a stall
that sells the funkiest slippers that make you feel that
you are walking on the moon. There is actually no other
way to describe it. There are no cartoon characters
unfortunately, but you might get away with wearing
them to work!

   PS They had a promotion on over the weekend, two
for the price of one, and they throw in a free scarf too.

⌐ **Wiesie**

Arty by London

Snap

Does anyone know any venues, preferably in south or central London, that allow amateur photographers and artists to display their work? *The Clapham Picture House* has an ongoing display in their bar, but there's quite a long waiting list. Are there any other places like this that anyone knows of?

Nixd

There is a display in Canary Wharf shopping centre under No.1 Canada Square that shows art from the local area and which is usually of a high standard. After seeing things displayed here I have often gone to the gallery or website where rest of the collection is displayed and I am sure others do too so try here. Otherwise the *Greenwich Union* shows artists and in Greenwich generally there are quite a few displays and things including an open-house weekend try googling Greenwich artists should come up with something. Oh, and to keep banging on about it, they are opening a new *Picture House* of the Clapham chain in Greenwich so you could get on the list early for a space in their display area.

Guilty Emma

Have you tried asking in local bars, cafes and restaurants? A lot of them are now showing art for sale on the wall and I often look to see if I can brighten up my flat with some. The benefits for them are that they don't have to fork out to decorate the place... not sure if they ask commission though.

💬 suj

The Waterfront pub in Streatham will allow you to display your wares on their wall. I even nearly bought one once!

💬 reetyre

Beauty

Like it says in *American Beauty*, you have to open your eyes to the beauty all around you. How many times have you walked through Tottenham Court Road station? Lots, I imagine, just like me. The other day I looked for what felt like the first time at the murals. They are amazing! Google tells me they were done when the station was refurbished in the 1980s and are by the artist Eduardo Paolozzi. There are 1000 square metres of them, which, by my calculation (assuming each tile is roughly 2 cm by 2 cm) equates to 2.5 million tiles. I tried Google to see how long it took to do but no luck. Any tube buffs out there know?

💬 Crouch Ender

Read

Of a summer's day I like to spend my lunch hour sitting in the sun reading a book. The Temple Gardens are a favourite spot. Come the winter though it's rather too cold to sit outside so I spend my lunch hour in shops instead of reading; as a result I become stupid and poor. Can anyone recommend a quiet place to sit and read a book of a lunchtime, somewhere within a 10–15 minute walk of Fleet Street ideally?

The Assassin Prince

Any of the museums or major art galleries. If you become a 'friend' of that particular institution there's sometimes a Friends' Room with comfy chairs as well as the usual bonuses of private viewings, free entry to exhibitions and so on.

Dr. Hyde

How about the St Bride Library, tucked away in the *St Bride Institute* just off Fleet Street? (www.stbride.org) It happens to be a world-class specialist library on all aspects of printing, from newspapers to typography to graphic design, but it is free to use, has friendly staff and a pretty reading room. If you want, I'm sure no one would notice you reading your own books, but you may enjoy reading about the history of Fleet Street itself, if not the development of Helvetica or Arial.

Scott

I recommend the City of London Library in Shoe Lane for a quiet lunch break. As an alternative, some of the City churches are open for lunchtime concerts; an example is St Martin's within Ludgate.

💬 pussinboots

Luxury

Anybody out there know of a fancy cinema at the 'luxury' end of the market where one can take one's partner or friends to watch a new film? I'm fed up of annoying kids spilling popcorn onto me in the multiplexes. Surely there is an alternative?

💬 Xpablo

The Everyman in Hampstead is now the swankiest of swanky cinemas with plush red seats, two-person 'love' seats, new 'club suites' (with foot stool) and a gallery with a bar and sofas. They have a room with a projection screen which can be hired for private parties.

💬 Jimmy J

Investigate the *Charlotte Street Hotel* too, and its sister, the *Covent Garden Hotel*. They're pricey, but they have small, amazingly plush screening rooms available for hire: www.firmdale.com/csh.html and click on 'Screening Room'.

💬 Dan

The Tricycle in Kilburn may meet your needs. It's a great cinema and free of the riff-raff that usually attend the chains.

💬 Silent Bob

Artbar

About six months ago I was dozily listening to BBC London late at night when someone was discussing a bar/club in London that provides paint and easels and allows patrons to drink and create a piece of art at the same time. I'm trying to organise a 'different' evening out for my friends (amiable 30/40 somethings) and would love to find out where this place is (if it still exists).

Genienitro

I recently spent an instructive Monday evening at _Notting Hill Arts Club_ (www.nottinghillartsclub.com) making a cat out of some pipecleaners and wool. It was a fiver in, but wine was £8 per bottle until 9pm, you got fizzy sweets and lollipops, creative advice from the organisers and there was a prize for the best cat created that evening. (Sadly, Tripod, my creation, didn't get the recognition she deserved.) They played some great tunes, the crowd was very mixed and it was open until 1am. Not having done anything creative in years it was surprisingly relaxing and restorative.

Mod

Fig108, in Westbourne Studios is your place. I took a group of 12 there last Saturday and it was _great_. The two organisers/artists were lovely and very supportive: 'Mmm, that green and brown looks great, you can put anything on top of that and it'll look really effective' to my horrible camouflage mess of murky colours. A couple

of our group turned out to be quite good but even
those who were really wary of the whole thing were fine
once they followed initial advice of 'pick a colour you
like and a brush/implement you like the look of and just
get some colour onto the white canvas'. Could go on for
ages as I thought it was great, but in short, do go, but be
warned that Westbourne Studios itself is a funny old place
a massive warehouse with staggeringly loud music,
filled with uber-cool west-London types. The *Fig108* studio
is in a room off that, so it is quieter, with mellow music,
very sociable and welcoming. But you do have to brave
the noise and queues to wash the paint off afterwards!
Other bit of advice I took a (civilised!) hen party,
and thought afterwards it might have been better as
an afternoon thing rather than evening. I think they're
flexible in when they can offer it. And I think £40/head
is a bargain!

💬 earch

Check them out at www.fig108.com and see the gallery
of previous efforts at various stages of drunkenness.
  Go, paint, enjoy.

💬 fluffy

Beyond London

Question for those travellers out there: with hindsight, what are some of the best gadgets (nothing too wanky) or little things you wished you had packed in your suitcase that just make travelling a little easier – my list currently starts with one of those torches you can strap on your head (most useful when hands-free mode needed in jungles at night); where to buy and all suggestions welcome.

💬 **Miss Itchy Feet**

I went to Central America two years ago for four months and had the most amazing time. The two niftiest things I packed, which I took only as an afterthought but came so much in handy, were a mossie net and duvet cover. Both mean you can be so much less picky over where you sleep: sleep IN the duvet cover so it's like a light sleeping bag; use it as picnic blanket etc. And a mosquito net means that you can ignore spiders on the walls etc. Enjoy the trip!

💬 **Lili**

Solid shampoo I got some from Lush. Lathers in any kind of water too, but not in a massive OTT foamy way, which helps. Pack things in small plastic zip lock bags from *Tesco*, cos they are super handy for the weirdest things. Including soggy bikinis when running to catch transport after day on beach. Or spare biltong (dried beef) for eating at any time, anywhere. Spare small padlocks with locks. Small bike lock with the plastic cover, preferably the thin light one.

Then the wanky bit... An iPod with all those tunes for all those times... never took one (they weren't invented) but would have loved to have small box of tunes... also... a kikoi, which is like a rough cotton version of a sarong, from Africa. Sarongs are crap, they are no use as towels or blankets and they slip off when you try and use them as clothing. Kikois are great towels, dry quickly, look much better and take up minimal space. Not sure where you'd get one though. Again, wanky, but my Birkenstocks were a godsend when I was travelling. Sweaty traveller feet don't like plastic, it rots. Nice. I think that's quite enough for now. Enjoy, I'm jealous!

💬 **aimee**

I found that a pair of earplugs were essential. I found guest houses in cities were always right by the noisiest roads, and all shared accommodation has a snorer. Helped me out a treat. They soon get disgustingly filthy, and you're probably likely to get an ear infection, but the good night's sleep is well worth it.

💬 **Grim**

Yes, a head torch is essential, as is a Swiss army knife (or even better, a Leatherman if the budget stretches that far). To that list I would add a sleeping sack silk ones can be quite expensive and in the heat cotton is often better so sewing a single sheet into a bag works well. Take a good stock of anti-diarrhoea tablets and when you get your shots from the doctor ask them to prescribe you some broad spectrum antibiotics in case of emergencies. Moist wipes are great for the jungle when there are no showers to be seen. Not sure of the best shops to buy outdoors stuff as I'm not from these parts but there are lots of places in Covent Garden.

💬 **Crusty**

Sandwich bags; take a roll of these, they're super handy. You can put wet stuff in to keep your other stuff dry, put dry stuff in to keep it dry, keep dust off any expensive gear (cameras and so on), use them as emergency gloves even, keep stuff you pick up or buy in (pretty stones off the beach for instance), use 'em as waterproof socks, put fruit and stuff in to keep clean and more or less fresh, and you can even keep sandwiches in them.

Baby wipes; get the super-cheap pound shop ones that are impregnated with alcohol, not the good ones with moisturiser. You can use these to clean just about anything from dirty windscreens, to cutlery, to your own sweaty body. And the alcohol helps to kill most nasties.

Hand sanitiser; get a little bottle from *Superdrug*. Handy for washing your hands when you've no water, and very refreshing on your face. Especially handy if you wear contacts and need to clean your hands to take them out.

A small bottle of iodine cleans tiny cuts that would otherwise get infected and you can use it to purify water too.

And best of all haemorrhoid cream. No really, this stuff is the best for insect bites or jellyfish stings. It has local anaesthetic so it stops itching, and it makes swelling go down. Wouldn't go anywhere without it.

💬 **Jon**

And finally

Church

Soon my Mum will be visiting me for the first time since I moved to London. She hasn't been here since years ago, when she remembers visiting a small church with lots of little boats hanging from all the walls and the ceiling (I think). It was dedicated to sailors and had a funny name. She gets quite nostalgic about it and I'd love to bring her there if it still exists... anyone seen it?

ally

I think that the church you and your mum is looking for is the All Hallows church near the Tower of London. Check out the link: www.hiddenlondon.com/all_hallows.htm.
   It is very cool but the ships are a little unnerving, like clog shops or olde world shops that only sell teddy bears!

Bobbers

I think the Church that you are looking for is St Clement Danes (Patron saint of Sailors) located in the middle (traffic island) of the Strand. Has more RAF stuff though than Navy, as in the '50s it was dedicated to the RAF.

Jannanni

Could it be Walthamstow's Lighthouse Methodist Church, 120 Markhouse Road, E17? It has a real lighthouse atop (instead of a belfry), and Waltham Forest's council says

'The whimsical Lighthouse turret reflects the nautical connections of its founder, Captain King of the Bullard line of steamers.' Unfortunately, not being a very churchy person, I can't attest as to whether the interior is as nautical as the exterior.

💬 **Dave**

The Ten Commandments

As chosen by the readers of the weekly London by London email.

I. Thou shalt treat all other Londoners as thou wouldst wish to be treated thyself.

II. Thou shalt have the courtesy to let passengers off the train before thou bargest on and taketh a prize seat.

III. Thou shalt have thy Travelcard/Oyster Card in thine hand when thou reachest the ticket barriers, and thou shalt not stand there, rummaging in thine bag for an hour.

Thou shalt not suddenly stop walking in the middle of Oxford Street simply because thou hast noticed a nice top in the window of Kookai.

 Thou shalt not operate an umbrella without proper training.

 Thou shalt not wear ye darke glasses underground. Ye nobs.

Though shalt make good and ready use of deodorant and other personal hygiene products, especially on hot days if thou needest to travel by tube.

Thou shalt talk quietly, or not at all, on thy mobile phone when on the bus – nobody else wants to hear what Emma did last night with Mark or how much thou didst spend on thy fucking shoes.

 Thou shalt harbour ridiculous and fathomless grudges about areas of the city which are not thine own. Until of course thou goest there to live.

 Thou shalt do something new every month.

And finally...
Thou shalt not use the words 'thou shalt' when writing commandments because the commandments were never written like that in the bible and we're pretty sure Charlton Heston never said it either.

Send us yours: www.londonbylondon.co.uk/ten

Acknowledgements

We would like to thank the following people for their contributions to London by London and for being part of the LBL community. Cheers!

Abi, absolutechaos, Adderface, aimee, AJH, Alastair, Albert, Alex, ally, andrew, Ang Ali, Anna, Anna's brother, ATP, auawsha, Audrey, Baastaard, babybat, Bad bwoy, bad girl bubby, Badger Kitten, badly dubbed boy, Bakerloo BadBoy, barmaid, BC The Geek, Beaver, Becksy boy, Beeg, belisha, beacon, Bella, Ben, Beryl Bouffe Schwede, Big Sis, Bill, billy, BillyGoat, birdbrain, Blonde Chick, Bobbers, bongo the clown, Boozehound, braindead geordie, Brendan, Brooce, Bruce, Brucey, Bunky, But having fun anyway!, Callan, calm as you like, Cardinal Richelieu, Caroline, Caroline393, Cazza, C-Bob, Chanted_snicker, Cheesemeister, cheesy rider, chelseagirl, Cherub, ChildoftheJago, Chorizo Boy!, Chris, Chris, Christoff van Rensburger, Chz, Claire, Clairey, classybird, Clefty, Coningsby, Cornholio, Cotal Tunt, cozmokaty, Crack Whore, crackers, Crazy Eddy, Crispy, crofty, Crouch Ender, Crusty, curry comber, Curry Monster, Daisy, dalziel, Dan, danny boy, Darling, Dave, davina, DB, Deb the regular cab-user, deefer, Delvin, desperate smoker, Desperately Seeking Some Latin, Dick Wittington, Dirtos, Dirty Sue, Dolly, dominic, Dorflbob, Dr Bone, Dr Spewan, Dr. Hyde, Dream Monkey, druster, Dumb Brunette, earch, east acton gal, East End Girl, Ed, ed~money, ede, El Guitarro, elaina, elena, Elton Stoney, Elvis' Burger, Emma, enfant terrible, Envman, Fabsal, faking girl, FilthBuster, Fleance, Flo, fluffy, fluffy mark, Food Fan, Food Man, 'Foreign Muck' Guy, Frank, Friendly Geek, Gaijingirl, Galeria Gonnorea, Garth, Gavin, Genienitro, Gilly, Ginger Badboy, ginger ninja, Giovanni, Giz, gizbourn, Gizzard, Gob-smacked, Goldhawk Gal, Good Girl, Griff, Grim, grumpy not so old woman, Grumpy Old Man, Guilty Emma, Hackney Girl, handsfree, Hannah, hannahbanana, Harri, Harriet, Health Freak, Hels, Hettie, Highbury Gal, Hocus Pocus, Honeybaby, Hong Kong Suey, Horsey Horserson, Hungry, I'd visit but I'd never live there, ils, injured, Ippy, IrisRed, Jannani, Jase, Jayc, JB, jcrw, jeane, Jenn, jennyliz, jerseygirl, Jezza, Jif, Jif, Jimmy J, JJ, Jodie, Jon, Jonesey, jonno, JooPoo, Juan Tan O'Mera, Juicy, Justonecornetto, K8LN, Kate, katjajulia, Kaymonster, Kenningtom, Kensal Green, kit, Konaboy, Laferge, Laurence, leapy, Leftie-nonsense-corrector, Less Gappy Than Before, Leytonstone Boy, Lifelonglondoner, Lili, Linda Palermo, Liner, Little G, Lizardbath, Llamapiss, loaf, lofty, Londoner on tour Down Under, londonplayboy, longterm, renta, Louise, Louise M, Lucky Layla, Lulu, Lupe, Mad King, MadKingSoup, Magpie, magpiepokinggeezer, mappeal, Mary, Matt A, Matthew, Maud, Maureen, Maxbiker, Metro Geek, mickyw, Mike, Mike (Mrs), mikecarterinlondon, mindtherat, mindy manilow, Minesapint, minicab, Miss Itchy

Feet, Miss Lake, Miss Moneypenny, MM, Mod, mommy, moomee, Moomintroll, Mr Ben, Mr Chat, Mr Sandling, Mr Sniffy, MrMINI, Mrs Beck, mudge, Muz, Nancy Drew, Nathan Barley, Natts, Neverbeenabletodunk, Newly Found Sister, ninorc, Nixd, north7, Not a NIMBY, nowlookhereyoungman, Office Mover, olhol, Oliver Lester, olly, once bitten, oops, Paperboat, part-timer, Paula, Pauly, pdr, pedal power, peelit, Pelepeg, Penelope Pitstop, Penfold, peshman, Pesk, Pete, Pete R, PeteFromPlaistow, Peter, phatflaresback, PhilG, piehead, pippart, Pixie, Plaistow Plasterer, pockettiger, Polly, Pop C, Popsickle, psaf, psaf, pussinboots, Pussycat, Rainy Tuesday, Raven, Recumbent Guy, Red, reetyre, reggae riot, RichardP, RichBowen, RichP, Riesie Mittens, RiverMan, Riz, Robo, robram, Roger, Ronnie, RP, ruby ru, Salty, Salty McPepper, Sam, samsid, Sassenach, Satiated, Satisfied?, scally, Scared and Broke, Scott, Scott Keir, sellers, SFULG, Shazza, Signorina, Silent Bob, Single gal in London, Skidoo, Sladey, smoothcheeks, snowjack, Sophie, spandangle, Spandangle, Spaniel, sparkleshark, speeler, Spike, Spotty David, Spyrone, Sqig (AKA mad crazy lady), Sqweno, stella, Stella Rimington, Stocky, strawberryfluff, Suckmonster, Suj, Superali, SuperFlake, sweetcheeks, Syzygy, talkative, Tash, Teefer, teepot, Terence, That Bloody Scotsman, The Assassin Prince, The Beak, the elephant man, the errorist, The extras, if wanted, The Mediator, The Pesk, The Secret Person, thecustardmonkey, TheMoff, thetotateeteetotaofeeyore, Thomas the Tanked Up Engine, Tiddles, Tim, TiredAndEmotional, Titus Goodlittle, TK, Toby, tom, Tomba, Tonytone, TonyW, Towerboy, Tree, tube driver, tubeangry, tubeguru, Tubeworm, Twiglet, Uptown Coil,

V, Viet-Knatt, vincentwong, WelshBird, whatever, Wiesiee, Will's sister, Willy, Winnersandlosers, Witness #01, Wonderferret, Wooden Horse, Woodster, WorldGirl, X marks the spot, Xpablo, yuri, Z, Zed, ZeroGravitas, Zogs.

Places worth a visit

_____
_____
_____
_____
_____
_____
_____
_____
_____
_____
_____
_____
_____
_____
_____
_____
_____
_____
_____

Places to avoid

_____
_____
_____
_____
_____
_____
_____
_____
_____
_____
_____
_____
_____
_____
_____
_____
_____
_____